Young Children's
Thinking

Education at SAGE

SAGE is a leading international publisher of journals, books, and electronic media for academic, educational, and professional markets.

Our education publishing includes:

- accessible and comprehensive texts for aspiring education professionals and practitioners looking to further their careers through continuing professional development

- inspirational advice and guidance for the classroom

- authoritative state of the art reference from the leading authors in the field

Find out more at: **www.sagepub.co.uk/education**

Young Children's Thinking

Los Angeles | London | New Delhi
Singapore | Washington DC

Marion Dowling

Los Angeles | London | New Delhi
Singapore | Washington DC

SAGE Publications Ltd
1 Oliver's Yard
55 City Road
London EC1Y 1SP

SAGE Publications Inc.
2455 Teller Road
Thousand Oaks, California 91320

SAGE Publications India Pvt Ltd
B 1/I 1 Mohan Cooperative Industrial Area
Mathura Road
New Delhi 110 044

SAGE Publications Asia-Pacific Pte Ltd
3 Church Street
#10-04 Samsung Hub
Singapore 049483

Editor: Marianne Lagrange
Editorial assistant: Kathryn Bromwich
Production editor: Thea Watson
Copyeditor: Sarah Bury
Proofreader: Jill Birch
Indexer: Anne Solamito
Marketing manager: Catherine Slinn
Cover design: Wendy Scott
Typeset by: C&M Digitals (P) Ltd, Chennai, India
Printed in India at Replika Press Pvt Ltd

Library of Congress Control Number: 2012930556

British Library Cataloguing in Publication data

A catalogue record for this book is available from the British Library

ISBN 978-1-4462-1095-6
ISBN 978-1-4462-1096-3 (pbk)

Contents

About the author   vii

Preface   viii

Acknowledgements   x

Glossary of terms   xi

1   Thinking about Young Children's Thinking   1

Our brains, minds and thoughts; Why it is important to consider
young children's thinking; What happens when children think?;
How we recognise young children's thinking; Main messages
in this chapter; References

2   Early Thoughts: Babies' and Infants' Thinking
     from Birth to Three Years   25

The receptive young brain; Feeling close, loved and secure;
Social understandings; The world of possibilities; Making sense;
Creating imaginary worlds; Communicating through behaviour
and language; Main messages in this chapter; References

3   How Close Adults can Support Babies'
     and Infants' Thinking   43

Relationships; Supporting very young children as thinkers
during transition; Companionship and communication;
Climate; Encouraging early intentions; Useful stories; References

4   Playing with Thoughts and Ideas: Young
     Children's Thinking 3–5 Years   70

Developing a disposition to think; Social understandings:
thinking with other children; Making sense; Communicating
thoughts through talk; Intentional thinking; Main messages
in this chapter; References

5   How Close Adults can Support Young Children's
    Thinking at 3–5 Years   97

Relationships; Supporting young children as thinkers during
transitions; Communication and companionship; Climate;
Promoting intentional thinking; Useful books; References

6   Brimming with Thoughts at Home and in
    School: Children's Thinking 5–7 Years   127

A shift in development; Maintaining a disposition to think;
Social understandings: thinking with friends and as one of
a group; Making sense; Sharing and sustaining thinking
through talk; Further insights into intentional thinking;
Main messages in this chapter; References

7   How Close Adults can Support Children's
    Thinking during the Early School Years   152

Relationships; Supporting children's transitions into
Key Stage 1; Communication and companionship; Climate;
Sustaining intentional thinking; Useful books; References

Index   182

About the author

 **Marion Dowling** has spent all of her wonderfully varied career working in Early Years.

She was involved in the early development of the playgroup movement, worked as head teacher of a state nursery school and as an adviser in two large shire authorities. As a member of Her Majesty's Inspectorate Marion gained a national perspective on provision for young children. Since 1995 she has worked independently as a consultant and trainer on local, national and international initiatives. All of her work is based on regular and frequent visits to early childhood settings.

Marion has published extensively in early years journals and is the author of several books. Her particular interests are linked to young children's personal, social and emotional development and children thinking. Marion has served on various advisory groups to the government. She was President and is now a Vice President of Early Education and has directed two Early Education Projects on *Exploring Young Children's Thinking*.

Preface

Once again the early years and primary phases of education are under scrutiny and new frameworks are being prepared to revise curriculum content. This book is more concerned, however, not with what young children learn, but rather with how they learn. It is heartening to see that the Tickell Review shares this concern and highlights young children 'creating and thinking critically' as one of three enduring characteristics of effective learning (1). This characteristic has been adopted in the new Statutory Framework for the Early Years Foundation Stage (2).

The term *Supporting Sustained Shared Thinking* is now commonly used in educational documents and in training; the term is derived from research findings which show that babies and young children gain in learning when their thinking is supported (3, 4). Many practitioners recognise this and have developed their practice accordingly. Case studies in the book affirm some of the sensitive and imaginative work that is taking place. These should be helpful to those who are less experienced in this aspect of pedagogy.

The book is intended for those studying for Early Years Practitioner Status, Early Childhood and Foundation degrees. It is also relevant to early years practitioners, teachers and teaching assistants. The current Independent Review of Early Education and Childcare Qualifications is considering how best to strengthen training, qualifications and career pathways for all those involved in the early years sector (5). Whatever the outcome, this book will be a useful resource for a range of practitioners involved in different aspects of continuing professional development where there is a focus on young children thinking.

I have (as always) aimed to link theory to practice. Chapter 1 sets out the territory around children's thinking and touches on many issues which are taken up in later chapters. Chapters, 2, 4 and 6 outline some of the main aspects of children's thinking at different stages of their lives. Chapters 3, 5 and 7 pick up on these aspects and signpost readers to ways in which they can support children and their parents.

Most parents want the very best for their children but they are not always aware of how their child's behaviour reflects their developing thoughts and ideas. I have included some practical suggestions for work with parents; however, the most important factor is to gain parents' interest and enthusiasm, respecting and helping them to recognise their powerful role in their child's development. Some parents appreciate this already, others need time and encouragement before they come on board. The distinction between different age groups is intended as a helpful guide. However, the chapters are not designed to be strictly age-specific; hence the deliberate overlaps between some age groups. Three year olds are referred to in both Chapters 2 and 4 and similarly 5 year olds are included in Chapters 4 and 6. I hope that this emphasises that children in one year group can be very different and reflect a range of development.

The remit of this book is ambitious – it covers a huge area and dips into some very complex issues. I have thoroughly enjoyed writing a book which covers such wide territory but inevitably I have fallen short. The overview of children's development as thinkers cannot be comprehensively covered here and the chapters on practice can often suggest only headlines for practical action. Despite this, I hope that readers are offered some insights into the wonders of how young minds develop and how close adults can support this process.

Access a selection of specially chosen SAGE journal articles here: www.sagepub.co.uk/dowling

References

1. Tickell, C. (2011) *The Early Years: Foundations for Life, Health and Learning.* Independent Report to HM Government on the Early Years Foundation Stage. London: Department of Education, p. 88.
2. Department for Education (DfE) (2012) *Statutory Framework for the Early Years Foundation Stage.* para 1.10, Cheshire: DfE (downloaded from the DfE website).
3. Sylva, K., Melhuish, E.C., Sammons, P., Siraj-Blatchford, I. and Taggart, B. (2004) *The Effective Provision of Pre-School Education (EPPE) Project: Technical Paper 12 – The Final Report: Effective Pre-School Education.* London: Department for Education and Skills/Institute of Education, University of London.
4. Siraj-Blatchford, I., Sylva, K., Muttchock, S., Giden, R. and Bell, D. (2002) *Researching Effective Pedagogy in the Early Years (REPEY).* DfES Research Report. London: Department for Education and Skills, p. 356.
5. Nutbrown, C. (2012) *The Independent Review on Qualifications in Early Education and Childcare.* London: Department for Education.

Acknowledgements

So many people have been involved in the production of this book and thanks are due particularly to Marianne Lagrange and Kathryn Bromwich at Sage. Several colleagues have been extremely generous in their preparedness to read and comment on drafts, among them Sharon Hogan, Maureen Lee and Kathy Brodie.

Thank you to Wingate Community Nursery School and Trimdon Grange Nursery and Infant School for providing wonderful examples of practice and also the families who have allowed me to share examples of their young children's thinking. Thanks also to Peter Dixon who shared the sparkly idea of introducing children to 'dragons' claws'.

Most of the case studies arise from my observations of young children over a number of years and some of these children have now moved away and are young adults. In all cases, their names have been changed apart from where they asked to keep their own name. Every effort has been made to obtain necessary permissions in regard to copyright material and I apologise if, inadvertently, any sources are unacknowledged.

Finally, thank you to my lovely grandchildren, who have provided some of the source material, and above all to my husband, Barry Allsop, who has given me constructive criticism, time and constant encouragement to write.

Glossary of terms

Definitions refer to meanings of these terms as they are used in the context of this book.

Attachment: the need for babies and young children to seek intimate relationships with their parents and other close adults who live and work with them.

Attunement: being on the same wavelength as the young child.

Companionship: an equal and familiar relationship between individuals which involves affection, shared interest and support.

Discrete methods: specific programmes and materials are used to teach specific thinking skills.

Early Years: the period of time from birth to the end of the academic year in which a child reaches five years of age.

Infused methods: everyday situations and scenarios are used to support children's thinking.

Key person(s): the named practitioner(s) with whom the child and close family members have the most contact. The key person approach involves a reciprocal trusting relationship between a member of staff and a family. The Early Years Foundation Stage (EYFS) requires that every child must have a key person (likely to be the child's special person).

Key Stage 1: covers Years 1 and 2 in primary school in England, when children are between five and seven years old.

Metacognition: thinking about thinking and consciously using different thinking strategies to solve problems.

Parents: mothers, fathers, other relatives who care for children and the primary carers of looked-after children.

Practitioner: any adult who works in an Early Years setting directly providing education and care for children.

Regulation: being controlled by another.

Re-presentation: replay, describe and make sense of experiences through different means (represent through moving, talking, making and marking).

Schema: repeated patterns of behaviour which children use in their play to explore and express their developing thoughts and ideas.

Self-regulation: being in charge of oneself; involves the ability to manage one's emotions, socialise with others and become an autonomous learner (thinker).

Special person/close person: one of a small number of adults in the home, setting or school who has developed a close relationship with a child.

Super-hero: a fictional character having extraordinary or superhuman strengths and powers.

Sustained, shared thinking: when two individuals work together on a shared enterprise which contributes to, develops and extends thinking.

Teacher: any trained adult (including teaching assistants) who works in a school to provide education and care for children from five to seven years.

Very young children: refers to babies and children up to three years.

Young children: refers to children from three to five years.

1

Thinking about Young Children's Thinking

Intentions

This chapter explores:

- what is thinking in young children
- why it is important to have regard for young children's thinking
- what happens when young children think
- how we recognise their thinking

Our brains, minds and thoughts

Brain and mind

We are all born with a physical brain but how does the mind develop? This is a vast and almost imponderable question but we know that the mind is more than the grey matter that we all inherit. Rather, it is shaped and refined by individual personal experience – as such, it is unique to each person. Susan Greenfield suggests that 'the mind may be the evolving personal aspect of the physical world' and 'consciousness brings the mind alive' (1). Young babies become conscious of and responsive to personal experiences from birth, in particular the loving interactions they have with close adults. Maria Robinson states that 'From this sensitive beginning of understanding the individual needs of the baby, there is also born the beginnings for the baby to have a mind of their own' (2).

We know that the young physical brain is very receptive to experience, and Gopnik and her colleagues liken a new baby's brain to a computer that is set up and running. This enables them to absorb experiences from their world and gradually start to make sense of them (3). Given these insights, Tricia David helpfully suggests that 'maybe if we use a computer analogy we can, for now, think of the brain as the hardware and the mind as the software' (4).

Thought

Defining thinking is equally difficult and particularly so as much research focuses only on 'thinking skills' (5, 6). The National Curriculum states that thinking involves the basic cognitive skills of perception (understanding), memory, concept formation (forming ideas), language and symbolisation (representations); these underpin the ability to reason, to learn and to solve problems (7). But any person familiar with young children knows that their thoughts and ideas are not only to do with intellectual development. As Robson points out in her comprehensive book, *Developing Thinking and Understanding in Young Children*: 'It is more than a skill. Equally important is the development of the disposition to make use of this skill, to want to be a thinker and to enjoy thinking' (8).

Thinking and learning

Some educationalists such as Claxton reject the term 'thinking' in favour of the broader term 'learning' (9). For the purposes of this book, I refer to young children thinking but not only in a narrow, rational sense. I link mind and thought, recognising that thinking results from processing all the experiences that are received in the mind. Peel summarised this over fifty years ago: 'Thinking is part of what goes on inside the mind, in between sense-reception and effective action' (10). When we apply this definition to young children and observe their behaviour, we recognise that their thinking is closely linked to early physical and sensory experiences, social growth and feelings and their creative powers. Thinking is closely involved with the whole child.

Why it is important to consider young children's thinking

Parents and practitioners living and working with children have always been faced (and sometimes fazed!) by young children's thoughts and ideas. Often we are amused and bemused by children's actions and comments but are not sure what they signify. In recent years there has been an upsurge of interest in issues around children's thinking. Why is it so high on our agenda for young children and what messages are we receiving? Some reasons are to do with:

- strong support from research evidence
- imperatives in National Frameworks
- increased insights from practitioners in their day-to-day work

Support from research evidence

During the last twenty-five years studies have recognised that thinking starts very early; young babies are primed to think in their unceasing efforts to make sense of the world. Parents have long known, for example, that their babies are aware of familiar faces and alert to stimulus – neuroscience now provides the evidence. Within the first year of life babies learn about others' minds and begin to recognise that when people disappear they have not gone for ever but still exist. Some of these points are highlighted in Chapter 1. Tricia David sums up powerful messages from the research she reviewed for *Birth to Three Matters*.

> Babies come already 'designed' or 'programmed' to be deeply interested in the people and world in which they find themselves. They are incredibly observant and selective, as well as being extremely clever at interpreting what they witness. They learn best by playing with things they find in their world and, above all, by playing with the familiar people who love them. (11)

Social contacts

Early studies starting with John Bowlby in the 1950s (12) and followed twenty years later by Mary Ainsworth (13) showed that babies and young children need close relationships to provide a secure base from which to explore the world. Sue Gerhardt's more recent work supports this with reference to neuroscience. She explores how early, loving contacts shape the baby's nervous system and suggests, for example, that being lovingly held is the greatest spur to development. Her work points up the importance of babies forming close attachments both with immediate family members and then a key person in daycare. These significant people are able to read a young child's behaviour and provide a tailor-made response to individual needs:

> Like a plant seedling, strong roots and good growth depend on environmental conditions, and this is most evident in the human infant's emotional capacities which are the least hard-wired in the animal kingdom, and the most influenced by experience. (14)

Around the same time as Mary Ainsworth, Lev Vygotsky's work showed that social relationships are not only important for emotional development, but are central to thinking and learning in the young brain. He regarded language exchanges as particularly significant in communicating meanings which a child can then use as the basis for his or her thinking (15). Barbara Rogoff builds on Vygotsky's theories and suggests that learning and thinking grow through guided participation with others (16). This might range from support and guidance from their special person to incidental contacts with family and play with friends.

Companionable learning and thinking

Rosemary Roberts introduces the notion of 'companionable learning', which, as she defines it, is very much to do with guided participation:

> Companionable learning is an essentially interactive process. The learners may not be learning the same things. ... But they will be jointly involved and focused; and companionably engaged, interacting with each other in the process of their learning together. (17)

Roberts outlines some principles of companionable learning which she claims support children's well-being. The principles are equally applicable in sustaining their thinking. The headlines below are adapted from Roberts' book, *Wellbeing from Birth*, and are expanded in subsequent chapters.

- First principle: companionable attention – young children gain full attention and are assured of their companion's continuing physical presence and interest
- Second principle: companionable play – children are engaged in play with close adults and peers
- Third principle: companionable conversations – children and close adults communicate through body language and talk
- Fourth principle: companionable apprenticeship – children and close adults do routine activities together, the child being regarded as a competent helper.

Communication is threaded across these four principles. It has been well researched in recent years (18, 19) and is a theme running through this book. Babies and infants use their bodies and facial gestures, in fact every means at their disposal, to reach out to close adults. The breakthrough to spoken language is a very significant step in thinking. Helen Moylett says that 'the process of dialogue with others mirrors our internal dialogue' (20). Because during the early years children use talk as a major tool to express their thoughts, parents and close adults have to listen carefully in order to appreciate what is being made public in young minds.

Making sense

Research has also helped us recognise that context or situation hold the key to the potential for children's thinking. Piaget made it clear that young children are not simply immature adults with undeveloped thinking mechanisms. He emphasised that children's thinking is qualitatively different but just as powerful as the thoughts of older people. The difference lies in them having less experience of life but using all their mental capacities to make sense of what they know. However, Piaget also held a somewhat inflexible view of young children; he believed that babies and children progress through distinct and fixed stages of development, for example, that children under seven years were not able to think in abstract ways but were entirely dependent on concrete experiences for understanding. This led practitioners to set a ceiling on children's abilities. During the 1960s and 1970s, when Piagetian thinking was most influential, a great deal of practice centred around waiting for individual children to achieve the next stage of readiness in their thinking rather than adults helping them to become ready (21).

These theories were radically extended by theorists such as Margaret Donaldson and David Wood, who opened our eyes to see that children are actually much more capable of higher levels of thinking if they are in situations which make sense to them (22, 23). Donaldson agreed with Piaget that formal and abstract thinking are simply not accessible to young children. Such thinking may involve theoretical situations or understanding and manipulating symbols. She suggested that this type of thinking is not linked to familiar and concrete situations. In this situation, young children will fail. However, rather than accept this deficient view, Donaldson suggested that if we offer young children opportunities to think or problems to solve which are linked or associated to known scenarios or to familiar stories, they show themselves to be significantly more competent.

Case Study 1.1

Raisa's dad complained to her nursery teacher that his daughter was not learning properly. He said that he had asked Raisa (3 years 7 months) to divide 9 by 3 – she had merely looked puzzled and walked away.

Jen, Raisa's teacher, gently explained that the little girl was in fact learning very well but needed to make sense of what was required of her and

(Continued)

(Continued)

to understand the language used. She persuaded Raisa's father to stay with his child for an hour in the nursery. During this time Raisa was happily engaged in domestic role-play with some dolls. Jen took a tin of nine cakes into the role-play area and suggested that these were a special treat and that Raisa should share the cakes fairly among the three dolls. Raisa shared out the cakes easily and equally.

Comment

Raisa was not able to solve a mathematical problem in the abstract. However, she was able to do so when the problem was associated with her play. She understood the use of language, 'share' and 'fairly', and could demonstrate her understanding through practical activity. Raisa's father began to understand how he could recognise his daughter's thinking and learning.

Importantly, we now understand that children's abilities to think are not static but are capable of development. Resnick suggests that young minds are better thought of as developing muscles than fixed-capacity engines (24). Given this, we face the challenge of how we support children's minds and their thoughts and ideas.

Infused and discrete methods to support thinking

There is still uncertainty about how we best support children to think. The two methods to promote thinking identified by Carol McGuiness are:

- 'infusion', where enhanced practice uses everyday situations and scenarios are used to help children identify and use their thinking;
- 'discrete', which uses specific materials, programme and techniques to introduce children to using different ways of thinking. (25)

A literature review from the NFER found that:

- when compared to discrete approaches, infused approaches to promoting children's thinking draw on a broader range of topics and, in particular, a broader variety of play
- when compared to infused approaches, discrete approaches to promoting children's thinking seem to encourage children to develop their abilities more systematically although the impact of discrete methods has not yet been evaluated properly. (26)

Despite the lack of hard evidence, conclusions about the limitations of one of these approaches are becoming clear. The main criticism of discrete teaching of skills is that it is narrow and fragmented and does not support children to transfer what they have learned to other contexts (27). Claxton supports this. He describes discrete approaches as 'bolt ons' – they may include lessons in teaching thinking skills or some handy suggestions to support memory or enquiry. Often the children enjoy these novel approaches but Claxton suggests that most discrete methods do not help children to use and apply their new found thinking to other situations (28).

The work of McGuiness and other theorists is mainly focused on approaches with older children. We must be aware that, in this book, we are considering what is right for babies and children at the start of their lives, and the terms 'infusion' and 'discrete' should be considered in this light.

The use of 'discrete' teaching materials and programmes are not relevant for very young children whereas 'infused' methods for babies and infants in the form of loving contacts, companionship and interested conversations will affirm their explorations and encourage thinking (see Chapter 3). Children of 3–5 years and in Reception classes will continue to benefit most from infused approaches, particularly in the opportunities offered to them in their self-chosen play and in their relationships and discussions with others (see Chapter 5). When children move into Years 1 and 2, infused approaches continue to be valuable while discrete programmes to support thinking, which are in accord with Donaldson's beliefs that children must make sense of what is offered, are also introduced (29). Some programmes, such as *Philosophy for Children* (30) and *Let's Think* (31), have been particularly successful in this respect and will be referred to in Chapter 7.

Thinking skills or dispositions

We are accustomed to refer to thinking as 'thinking skills', and of course we must support children's cognitive processes from the earliest age. But the reference to skills does not sit comfortably with a focus on the whole child. With young children it seems more relevant to refer to dispositions to think. Lillian Katz made the distinction: 'Dispositions are a very different type of learning from skills and knowledge. They can be thought of as "habits of mind", tendencies to respond to situations in certain ways' (32). We can of course teach an isolated skill such as categorising, but it's not much use if a child is not inclined to categorise things or people in everyday play or when going outside to explore. Moreover, whereas specific thinking skills may be taught successfully later in life, if a young child has been brought up to be compliant and accepting and strongly dissuaded to use his thinking abilities, it is extremely difficult to motivate him to do so later on. Thinking is hard work – it can mean feeling muddled, unsure, insecure and perhaps unsafe. It means breaking new ground and being brave enough to come up with your own ideas. In order to venture into this territory children have to be prepared to take a risk.

We know that the way in which we feel about ourselves has a powerful effect on the way we operate and this applies from the earliest years of life. If a four year old hasn't been cared for or respected as a human being, he feels that he isn't worth much and the chances are that in the reception class he will sink into his shell and become invisible. In his class, though, there will be other children who are naturally curious, relish challenge and problem solving, and grappling with ideas. Carol Dweck's work on *Mindsets* (33), explored in later chapters, highlights the significance of children's habits of mind and the way it influences their thoughts and ideas.

Margaret Carr's approach to assessment is focused on dispositions in young children and she asks the critical question 'How can eager learning be described and encouraged?' She explores this by suggesting important aspects of dispositions:

- becoming interested
- getting involved
- persevering with problems
- sharing ideas and thoughts with others.

Carr highlights one of these aspects with a Learning Story for four year-old Sean in which he persists with a difficult task even when he gets 'stuck'. Attached to this story is a photo of Sean using a carpentry drill. The teacher, Annette, records the incident:

> 'The bit's too small Annette, get a bigger one'. We do drill a hole and then use the drill to put in the screw. 'What screwdriver do we need?', asks Sean. 'The flat one.' Sean chooses the correct one and tries to use it. 'It's stuck.' He kept on trying even though it was difficult.

Carr explains that this Learning Story will provide a focus for more discussion between Annette and Sean and, together with other Learning Stories, helps both of them to see how well he is progressing in persevering with problems (34).

Strengthening dispositions to think

If we are serious about strengthening young children's dispositions to think, we should consider the influence of the environment – where is the scope for thinking? Claxton and Carr identify four backgrounds:

- a *prohibiting environment* may be tightly controlled with a predetermined schedule which makes it very difficult for children to make a response
- an *affording environment* offers some opportunities for children to become involved but not sufficient for all; there may be some intriguing aspects to explore but children are not made aware of them and only the most determined individuals will take advantage of what is there
- an *inviting environment* positively encourages children to ask questions and to work and play together
- a *potentiating environment* is likely to promote shared play activities where children take responsibility for decisions and power is shared with close adults (35).

Robson and Hargreaves' research into the beliefs and practices of practitioners in regard to young children's thinking also emphasises the importance of the environment and climate. Some main findings from their investigations include:

- the need for support for thinking to be woven into the child's daily experience rather than treated as something to teach separately (an infused approach as described by McGuiness)
- the benefits of outdoor experiences to provide children with opportunities to explore, investigate and problem-solve
- the importance of provision for play-based learning
- opportunities for children to make choices (also emphasised as a feature in Claxton and Carr's potentiating environment)
- the size of the group
- time given for children to practise and apply their ideas and to share them with others (36).

These important points are taken further in subsequent chapters.

Long-term benefits of supporting young children's thinking

Research findings are also providing encouraging messages about the value of adults supporting children's thinking and the long-term gains. Two major research projects, EPPE (*Effective Provision of Pre-School Education*) and REPEY (*Researching Effective Pedagogy in the Early Years*), considered a range of pre-school provision for children ages 3–5 and which factors had a positive impact on their learning (37, 38). Findings suggested that one of the ways in which we could identify high-quality early years practice was where children were helped to improve their thinking skills. In the most effective early years settings, staff provided opportunities to sustain and challenge children's thinking and to model this for children to share their thoughts with other children. The two projects and, in particular, the term 'sustained, shared thinking' were widely disseminated. It was defined as: 'an episode in which two or more individuals "work together" in an intellectual way to solve a problem, clarify a concept, evaluate activities, extend a narrative etc. Both parties must contribute to the thinking and it must develop and extend' (39).

Since then the EPPE project has followed the same children from pre-school into the primary school and now into the secondary sector (40). The primary study of children aged 3–11 found that by the end of Year 5 these older children had continued to benefit from attending high-quality and effective early years provision and this was reflected in their achievements in mathematics and reading. Moreover, the benefits were stronger where effective early years provision was followed by experiences in an effective primary school. This was particularly noticeable for the most vulnerable groups of young children who have had a poor start to life. The EPPE findings also recognise the strong influence of home and stresses that the greatest impact on children's progress is likely to be improving the quality of learning (which includes encouraging children's thinking) in both the home and early years and primary settings.

Although findings from this study are cautious, they are immensely encouraging in that we can see that by continuing to support children's thinking in early years and primary school as well as in the home, we are aiding their long-term achievements and importantly helping to make a difference to children who need it most.

Imperatives in National Frameworks

Within the last thirteen years children's thinking has been publicly highlighted in national policy documents across the United Kingdom.

Since 1999 thinking skills have been included in the National Curriculum. Thinking skills are expected to be developed at all key stages (41). In 2006, The Primary Framework for Literacy suggested core learning in Literacy that most children should achieve year by year. Many of these involve aspects of thinking. For example, in drama year one, children are expected to discuss why they like a performance; when engaging with and responding to texts in year two, most children are expected to give some reasons why things happen or characters change (42).

A little later, Early Years National Frameworks in England and Wales, Scotland and Northern Ireland give clear statements about the need to have regard to and offer support for young children's thinking. The Frameworks emphasise the importance of active learning, problem solving, inclusion and the need to provide learning opportunities which are tailor-made for each child. This means that practitioners must identify a child's interests and thoughts at the heart of all they plan and provide.

England

In England, the Early Years Foundation Stage, which refers to children from birth to five years, has been revised and the new Framework will be implemented in September 2012.

The government has accepted many of the recommendations from Clare Tickell's independent report and there are some clear messages in the new Framework which relate to young children's thinking. They are highlighted particularly in one of the three Characteristics of Effective Teaching and Learning:

- Creating and thinking critically is achieved where children
  - o 'have and develop their own ideas
  - o make links between ideas and
  - o develop strategies for doing things' (43).

The two other characteristics are:

- Playing and exploring
- Active learning

The messages in creating and thinking critically refer to fundamental ways in which children cultivate and use thoughts and ideas; namely, children's drive to be creative, categorise and connect, and start to control their thinking.

These messages are important but they are contained in a mere bullet point in the Framework and do not do justice to the essential role that children's thinking plays in their total learning and well-being.

Clare Tickell's report provides more detail by giving a rationale behind the three characteristics of effective learning which she describes as relating to 'lifelong learning' and 'about how rather than what children learn' (44). Tickell emphasises, though, that we cannot describe these in a developmental sequence. For example, a young baby may be very innovative in the way he plays with a soft toy and perseveres with this play activity, whereas a six year old may be at a loss as to how he might use additional resources to extend his construction and quickly loses interest in the activity. These characteristics apply to all children but will be demonstrated in different ways and at different times.

The new Framework follows Tickell's recommendation that practitioners should be mindful of how the characteristics support learning across the newly devised seven areas of learning. Moreover, in each of the prime and specific areas of learning there are references to children's thinking, for example:

- **Personal and social development – children:**
  - talk about their ideas and choose resources they need for their chosen activity
  - talk about their own and others' behaviour and its consequences
  - take account of one another's ideas about how to organise an activity
- **Communication and language**
  - Children listen to stories, accurately anticipating key events and respond to what they hear with relevant comments, questions or actions
- **Physical development**
  - Children move confidently in a range of ways, safely negotiating space
- **Mathematics**
  - Children solve problems, including doubling, halving and sharing
- **Expressive arts and design**
  - Children use what they have learned about media and materials in original ways. They represent their own ideas, thoughts and feelings through design and technology, art, music, dance, role play and stories (45).

Wales

The Welsh Assembly Foundation Phase Framework for Children's Learning, which covers children aged 3–7 years, includes developing their thinking as part of a non-statutory Skills Framework, which also applies across all of the areas of learning. The emphasis is on processes of planning, developing and reflecting, which help children acquire deeper understanding when they explore and make sense of their world. The statement for the Foundation Stage emphasises that these processes support children to think critically and creatively. Moreover, the processes should not be seen as separate and distinct, but should link together. Young children are initially impulsive but as they mature, and with support, they can be encouraged to adopt a more considered approach and learn from their experiences (46).

Scotland

In Scotland, Curriculum for Excellence became a mandatory document for ages 3–18 years in 2010. Before that, the early years and primary phases had been working to achieve requirements using guidance published in 2007. Building the Curriculum 2 identifies the main components within the main Framework, one of which is active learning. Practitioners are encouraged to support young children to learn actively, through playing together, tackling problems, extending communication skills and taking part in sustained, shared thinking (47).

Northern Ireland

The revised curriculum for Northern Ireland was introduced in 2007. Thinking skills and personal capabilities are considered to be at the heart of the curriculum for all phases of education and apply equally to children aged 4–7 years. The framework involves five strands:

- managing information
- thinking, problem solving and decision making
- being creative
- working with others
- self-management

In common with the other frameworks, these different types of thinking are intended to be integrated and infused across the curriculum and include every child (48).

Taken together, these national documents across the four countries of the United Kingdom offer consistent and clear messages regarding the importance of young children developing as thinkers. Practitioners and teachers need to seriously regard how to support them.

Increased insights from practitioners in their day-to-day work

These research findings and requirements in National Frameworks, which point up the significance of young children's thinking, really re-enforce what so many practitioners have intuitively long known to be true. Part of the Early Education Projects on Young Children Thinking (49, 50) involved structured discussions with those who are in daily contact with babies and young children in settings and reception classes, and this section summarises some of their views on the importance of the topic.

Need to focus more on children rather than pre-planned provision

In recent years those who work directly with young children have been required to give priority to planning and 'delivering' the curriculum. In their hearts, practitioners recognise that in these endeavours to *provide* for children they may be in danger of missing what children are interested in here and now, and where they are investing their energies. A carefully planned and resourced project on fairy stories may attract the attention of some reception children, but others are not sufficiently motivated when their minds are full of the latest super-hero character. We cannot make children learn but we can provide circumstances which entice their thoughts and ideas.

Gain a true picture of children's thinking competencies

Practitioners also recognise that, unless we have insights into ways in which children express their ideas and thoughts, we may be in danger of underestimating their potential for learning. Commonly, we look at children's mark making as an indicator of their achievement. However, a child may have poorly developed fine motor skills, he may have little pencil control and his drawings, paintings and models are immature. In this case, the representations may not reflect that child's complex and original ideas, which perhaps are revealed in role play or when he is engaged in constructing outside.

Case Study 1.2

Rachel, the reception teacher, had a class of 30 children and only a part-time teaching assistant. She found it difficult to observe children regularly in their self-chosen play.

At the start of the summer term Rachel was busy completing the profile statements for her class. She had become anxious about Carlos and his low scores in Communication, Language and Literacy (CLL). He was not interested in mark making in any form inside or outside, and Rachel had very few responses from him when she tried to engage him in conversation. He seemed to flit around different activities and found it particularly difficult to engage in any group activity.

Rachel decided to observe Carlos for longer periods to see if he performed differently in other activities.

She observed that Carlos engaged in construction with blocks; he was intent on building a snooker table and had attracted a group of boys who wanted to help and to play the game. It quickly became clear that Carlos was very conversant with the rules of playing snooker and he assumed the role of the expert. Carlos directed the boys to find two small balls and some wooden broom handles for cues. He explained the rules clearly and lucidly and organised a rota for taking turns. One of the boys complained that he couldn't remember when it was going to be his turn. Carlos calmly collected a large piece of paper. He asked each boy to give him the first letter of their name and made a list which showed the sequence for the players.

Comment

Rachel's observation of Carlos had revealed his interest in snooker. Given the opportunity to re-present the game and share his expertise with others, Carlos revealed competencies of which Rachel had previously been quite unaware. He was totally absorbed in the activity, used language to express his ideas and easily conveyed the rules to others through written recording.

Thinking underpins future achievements

Practitioners also know first-hand from their practice that where young children are good thinkers this is a precursor to later achievement. In order to write clearly and imaginatively and solve problems by using and applying mathematics at Key Stage 1 children must first become clear and inventive thinkers. If young children learn to reflect on their actions and recognise the link between cause and effect, they start to regulate their behaviour and are less likely to act impulsively – surely a lesson for life. Above all, children who are encouraged and become able to think for themselves are likely to become eager and autonomous learners. Those who work with young children on a day-to-day basis recognise that by supporting their thinking we are going with the grain of their learning and well-being; there are tangible signs of children being in their element and progressing their thoughts and ideas. Conversely, if we ignore children's interests and insist that they fit in with our ideas and programmes, we are in danger of going against the grain. This is hard work for both children and adults. Children have their own thoughts, but we can provide conditions which entice their ideas and help to grow their minds.

What happens when children think?

Mental disequilibrium

We can be going about our daily affairs cheerfully until we come up against something new that causes us to pause for thought. It may be as a result of a film we see, a book we read, a training course we attend or simply a discussion with a friend. Whatever the source, it poses a new idea or thought which doesn't quite fit in with what we know already.

It challenges our current understanding and we are not clear in our minds about it. What often follows is a period of confusion, often quite uncomfortable, as we try to gain a clearer understanding of this new notion. We may re-read part of the book, talk to others who have also seen the film, look again at the notes from our training or seek out the person we had the discussion with and ask her to explain her idea again. Over time, when we turn the idea over in our minds, we come to absorb or assimilate the new idea. Our former understandings are now no longer sufficient. They have to be modified in order for us to mentally adjust and accommodate to new thinking. As we accommodate to a new idea, the state of confusion or mental disequilibrium is resolved and, armed with new thinking, we have once more achieved a state of equilibrium.

Piaget developed the concept of the three processes of assimilation, accommodation and equilibrium as central to propel children's thinking forward, but it is also relevant for us all through life (51).

Being developmentally ready

We cannot force new thinking. It can take considerable time for a young child to give up her current understanding and adjust to a new idea. Sometimes a child is not developmentally ready to make a leap in her thinking. Piaget suggested that there is little that anyone can do to hurry this development and to some extent this is true. For example, a young child in a reception class will insist that shopkeepers give you money, not change. No lesson or explanation will alter this belief. But, as pointed out earlier, children are social creatures and also learn through active experiences. Given plenty of encounters with and conversations about role-play shopping with an adult or more experienced child and going shopping at home (to shops where cash is exchanged rather than card transactions!), the child is helped to move on through assimilating the notion of exchange, accommodating it and modifying her thinking (equilibrium).

Making connections

Young children are actively involved in trying to make sense of their world. They are buzzing with ideas. Given a rich environment and an adult who is a thinking companion, children will link or connect ideas together. One of the most exciting aspects of working with young children is to be present when they relate their thoughts, put two and two together and, through the processes of assimilation and accommodation, they arrive at a new point in learning.

Case Study 1.3

The practitioner read the story of *Harry the Dirty Dog*. Leon (3 years 6 months) usually found it difficult to listen to a story in a group. On this occasion, though, he listened intently and then a beam spread over his face. 'That's like my dog at home', he said excitedly, 'Sadie is like Harry – she is always getting dirty and we have to give her a bath.'

Comment

When listening to the story, Leon recalled his dog at home. He made a connection with the characteristics of the book character and Sadie. Immediately, the story made sense to him.

How we recognise young children's thinking

It is relatively easy to find out what older children think. We can read a piece of writing from a ten year-old child and recognise if they have understood the sequence and structure of a story. We may ask an eight year old how they arrived at their conclusion to a problem-solving activity. Even if their response is hesitant and incomplete, it still gives us insights into the child's thinking processes. Because younger children do not have this facility with written or spoken language practitioners and parents are alert to other clues.

Schema

Young children's thinking is heavily influenced by their interests and when they play freely they often repeat actions again and again. These repeated patterns of play can often (but not always) be recognised as a child's pre-occupation, or scheme of thinking, a term first used in 1953 by Piaget (52) and later used by Chris Athey in the Froebel Early Education Project (53). Children's common schemes of thought are listed and referred to in subsequent chapters. Recognising them is a helpful way of interpreting and understanding young children's sometimes puzzling behaviour. For example, we may observe children apparently flitting from activity to activity in a seemingly meaningless manner. Once we are familiar with different schemes of thinking, we may be able to interpret this behaviour and recognise that the apparent 'flitting' is the child's way of fitting his experiences together.

Case Study 1.4

Kwame, just three years old, is very active for every moment of his nursery session. He enters the role-play area and throws two teddies into the air – on to construction where he knocks over a tower of blocks which has been painstakingly constructed by two other boys. Kwame shouts 'great, great', before swiftly moving outside, clambering on to a wall and jumping off. This is repeated several times until he spies some balls. He rushes over and throws them high, shouting with glee as one lands on the roof of the building. Kwame looks around and then makes for a small grassy slope; he rushes up and down again and again before stopping at the bottom of the slope to pause for breath. Kwame then moves over to a box of dressing up clothes, clambers inside the box and covers himself with a curtain. He remains there for some time before climbing out but still wrapped in the curtain. He finds the wooden hidey hole and curls up inside.

Comment

Over the last two months, Kwame has shown this obsession for moving himself and objects (through kicking and throwing) in straight lines and arcs. His key person recognises that this behaviour shows a dominant trajectory schema and has encouraged Kwame to spend as much time as possible outdoors, which allows him scope for his schema while creating minimum disruption to others. Kwame now appears to be assimilating a new enveloping scheme which his key person supports by suggesting that she and Kwame build a special den for him to hide in the bushes. Kwame's interest in trajectory schema remains, particularly in kicking and throwing balls but his main pre-occupation is now hiding himself and two teddies in the new den.

We can also see how children's thinking through schema progresses.

- Fragile schemes of thought are observed as a baby shows interest in particular patterns of activity (pulling toys round in circles, dropping things from a height, sitting toys in rows).
- The schemes of thought are strengthened as the baby repeats the activity in different situations (starting to draw circles in the sand, jumping or dropping themselves from a height, separating and lining up his food on a plate).
- One scheme is co-ordinated with others through Piaget's processes of assimilation, accommodation and equilibrium to form a cluster of schemes.
- In turn, these increasingly complex clusters of schema develop as concepts. Schema are discussed further in Chapters 2, 4 and 6.

Re-presentations of their experiences

Children have different ways of re-presenting their experiences and making sense of them. Jerome Bruner suggests that children's re-presentations take three forms:

- through their physical actions – **enactive re-presentation**
- in their mark making, drawings and paintings – **iconic re-presentation**
- when they use symbols in their play, early writing and mathematics – **symbolic re-presentation** (54).

These three forms move from active to abstract ways of representing. Initially, babies and infants will use their bodies to represent what they understand. As children develop and mature, they show us more through mark making and by using symbols. However, Bruner suggests that all forms are equally valid and children will use them to suit their purposes. A four year old who has observed newly hatched frogs jumping in the nursery pond may:

- re-enact this experience through practising jumping herself from different surfaces (enactive)
- re-present through a drawing showing the frog's movement in twirls and swirls (iconic)
- build a pond using blocks and fabrics for water and use small-scale figures of frogs to re-play their jumping (symbolic).

Questions and comments

Young children also communicate their thoughts, ideas and enquiries through language. Babies use body language, eye contact and gesture to gain information, and their questions are clearly conveyed when they point to an object and confront the adult with searching look. With the emergence of talk, infants give us further insights into their enquiries.

Children are required to develop questioning skills in the National Curriculum and undoubtedly they can be helped to improve the quality and scope of their questions. However, young children will naturally ask questions if they want to know about something and if they are in a familiar environment. This is very apparent in the home where typically children inundate their family members with questions. Robson suggests that: 'one of the ways in which children seek to close the gaps in their experience is through asking questions. Children's questions reveal a lot about what they do and do not understand, their misconceptions and their interests. Their questions may not, however, all require an answer. What children may often be doing is using their own questions to help them to shape and clarify their thinking by thinking aloud'. (55)

Children around three years will also talk or drop comments about something which give us insights into their understandings and what is on their minds. Sometimes their contributions seem odd and not relevant to what is being discussed but there is always a connection.

Listening to children's questions and comments helps to illuminate some of their struggles with understanding difficult and emotional issues.

Case Study 1.5

Three year old Seb, sharing a group conversation in class about birds children had spotted in the garden, suddenly announced that boys didn't need mummies. His teacher quietly acknowledged that this was an interesting thought that perhaps Seb would like to chat about later. At the end of the afternoon Seb's childminder collected him and told her that Seb's mum had suddenly left the family at the weekend. It transpired that Seb's older brother had tried to console Seb by telling him firmly that the two boys and their dad could cope very well together. After all, boys and men did not need mummies.

Comment

Seb's comment about not needing mummies was expressed at a time when he was upset, confused and trying to convince himself of the wisdom of his brother's counsel. At this time he desperately needed to make a public statement.

In private conversations

In my experience, by the time they go to school it is not common for young children to be so open. Adults who are experienced in working with young children usually agree that their responses and comments in an adult-directed group are very different from the verbal exchanges that take place when children believe that they are conversing in private. Where an adult is perceived to be leading the conversation, children tend to be socially compliant. While a few confident individuals will speak unreservedly, many more will be more guarded with their responses, trying to sense what the adult wants to hear. However, these inhibitions and social constraints disappear when your children believe that they are out of earshot. Peer conversations flow on diverse topics and frank opinions are exchanged. Because they feel comfortable and at ease on their own territory with their talking partners, children appear less hesitant in their use of language.

They use words to express their ideas and differences of opinion, argue a point and seek clarification. Preserving the child's impression of privacy is essential, but adults who listen in unobtrusively will gain rich evidence of children's mindfulness.

Case Study 1.6

Here is a conversation between two boys playing with small world superhero figures.

Ricki: 'My dad's really tough – he's a wrestler and he can push people over, even my uncle Jack.'

Don: 'It's not good to fight people – my dad says you have to try to be friends.'

Ricki: 'Well... well, wrestling's not fighting, not really, my dad says it's a game.'

Don: 'Does your dad hurt people though?'

Ricki: 'Well only sometimes I think – but it's not proper fighting if it's a game. Some fighting you even kill people.'

Don: 'Mrs Evans don't like fighting, does she – does she like wrestling?' [Ricki shakes his head vigorously]

Comment

A thoughtful discussion where the boys try to distinguish between fighting and wrestling. They are aware of Mrs Evans' (their teacher) disapproval of violence and would probably not have this conversation in her presence.

Main messages in this chapter

- The importance of having regard for children's thinking is highlighted in National Frameworks, research evidence and reflected in the views of practitioners.
- Thinking involves the whole child and is strengthened through close relationships and real, motivating experiences.
- Young children's thinking is best developed through weaving support into their daily activities.
- Early support for their thinking can have long-term benefits.
- When young children think, they assimilate and accommodate new ideas and make connections to come up with a new notion in learning.

- Children demonstrate their thoughts through schematic behaviour, their re-presentations, questions and comments.

References

1. Greenfield, S. (1997) *The Human Brain*. London: Weidenfeld and Nicolson, p. 149.
2. Robinson, M. (2009) *The Wonder Year: 1st Year Development and Shaping the Brain*. Newcastle upon Tyne: Siren Films Ltd.
3. Gopnik, A., Melzoff, A. and Kuhl, P. (1999) *How Babies Think: The Science of Childhood*. London: Weidenfeld and Nicolson.
4. David, T., Gouch, K., Powell, S. and Abbott, L. (2003) *Birth to Three Matters: A Review of the Literature*. London: Department for Education and Skills (DfES), p. 117.
5. McGuiness, C. (1999) *From Thinking Skills to Thinking Classrooms*. DfEE Research Brief 115. London: Department for Education and Employment (DfEE).
6. Taggart, G., Ridley, K., Rudd, P. and Benefield, P. (2005) *Thinking Skills in the Early Years: A Literature Review*. Slough: NFER.
7. Department for Education and Employment (DfEE/Qualification and Curriculum Authority (QCA)) (1999) *The National Curriculum: Handbook for Primary Teachers in England*. London: Qualification and Curriculum Authority (www.nc.uk.net).
8. Robson, S. (2006) *Developing Thinking and Understanding in Young Children*. London: Routledge, p. 2.
9. Claxton, G. (2008) 'Cultivating Positive Learning Dispositions', available online at www.guyclaxton.com/publications.htm.
10. Peel, E.A. (1967) *The Pupil's Thinking*. London: Oldbourne, p. 11.
11. David et al. (2003) *Birth to Three Matters* (see note 4), p. 143.
12. Bowlby, J. (1953) *Childcare and the Growth of Love*. London: Penguin.
13. Ainsworth, M.D.S., Blear, M.C., Wakes, E. and Stayton, D. (1978) *Patterns of Attachment: A Psychological Study of the Strange Situation*. NJ: Lawrence Erlbaum Associates.
14. Gerhardt, S. (2004) *Why Love Matters*. London: Brunner-Routledge, p. 19.
15. Vygotsky, L. (1978) *Mind in Society*. Cambridge, MA: Harvard University Press.
16. Rogoff, B. (1990) *Apprenticeship in Thinking: Cognitive Development in a Social Context*. Oxford: Oxford University Press, p. 97.
17. Roberts, R. (2010) *Wellbeing from Birth*. London: Sage, p. 56.
18. David et al. (2003) *Birth to Three Matters* (see note 4), pp. 70–86.
19. Roulstone, S., Law, J., Rush, R., Clegg, J. and Peters, T. (2011) *Investigating the Role of Language in Children's Educational Outcomes*. DfE Research Report 134. London: Department of Education.
20. Moylett, H. (2011) 'Time to Talk', in *Nursery Education*, 13(1): 15.
21. Piaget, J. and Inhelder, B. (1969) *The Psychology of the Child*. New York: Basic Books.
22. Donaldson, M. (1978) *Children's Minds*. London: Fontana.
23. Wood, D. (1998) *How Children Think and Learn*. Oxford: Blackwells.

24. Resnick, L. (1999) 'Making America Smarter', *Education Week Century Series*, 18(30), pp. 38–40. www.edweek.org/ew/vol18/40resnick.h18.
25. McGuiness (1999) *From Thinking Skills to Thinking Classrooms* (see note 5).
26. Taggart et al. (2005) *Thinking Skills in the Early Years* (see note 6), p. vi.
27. Coles, M.J. and Robinson, W.D. (1991) 'Teaching Thinking: What is it? Is it Possible?', in M.J. Coles and W.D. Robinson (eds), *Teaching Thinking: A Survey of Programmes in Education*. London: Bristol Classical Press, pp. 9–24.
28. Claxton (2008) 'Cultivating Positive Learning Dispositions' (see note 9).
29. Donaldson (1978) *Children's Minds* (see note 22).
30. Lipman, M. (2003) *Thinking in Education* (2nd edn). Cambridge: Cambridge University Press.
31. Robertson, A. (2004) 'Let's Think! Two Years On', *Primary Science Review*, 82: 4–7.
32. Katz, L. (1988) 'What Should Young Children Be Doing?', *American Educator*, Summer: 29–45.
33. Dweck, C. (2008) *Mindsets*. New York: Ballentine Books.
34. Carr, M. (2001) *Assessment in Early Childhood Settings: Learning Stories*. London: Paul Chapman, p. 23.
35. Claxton, C. and Carr, M. (2004) 'A Framework for Teaching Learning: The Dynamics of Disposition', *Early Years*, 24(1), March: 87–97.
36. Robson, S. and Hargreaves, D. (2005) 'What Do Early Childhood Practitioners Think about Young Children's Thinking?', *European Early Childhood Research Journal*, 13(1): 81–96.
37. Sylva, K., Melhuish, E.C., Sammons, P., Siraj-Blatchford, I. and Taggart, B. (2004) *The Effective Provision of Pre-School Education (EPPE) Project: Technical Paper 12 – The Final Report: Effective Pre-School Education*. London: DfES/ Institute of Education, University of London.
38. Siraj-Blatchford, I., Sylva, K., Muttchock, S., Giden, R. and Bell, D. (2002) *Researching Effective Pedagogy in the Early Years (REPEY)*. DfES Research Report 356. London: DfES.
39. Ibid.
40. Sammons, P., Sylva, K. et al. (2007) *EPPE (3–11) Influences on Children's Attainment and Progress in Key Stage 2: Cognitive Outcomes in Year 5*. Research Brief No.: RB828 February 2007.D. London: DfES.
41. DfEE/QCA (1999) *The National Curriculum* (see note 7).
42. Department for Education and Skills (DfES) (2006) *Primary Framework for Literacy and Mathematics*. London: DfES, pp. 24, 26.
43. Department for Education (DfE) (2012) *Statutory Framework for the Early Years Foundation Stage*. Draft for Consultation. London: DfE, para.1.10.
44. Tickell, Dame C. (2011) *The Early Years: Foundations for Life, Health and Learning*. Independent Report to HM Government. London: DfE, pp. 87, 88.
45. Department for Education (2012) *Statutory Framework for the Early Years Foundation Stage* (see note 43), para 1.13.
46. Department for Education, Lifelong Learning and Skills (2008) *Foundation Phase: Framework for Children's Learning*. Cardiff: Welsh Assembly Government.
47. Learning and Teaching Scotland (2007) *Building the Curriculum 2: Active Learning in the Early Years*. www.ltscotland.org.uk/building your curriculum/ policy content.

48. Northern Ireland Curriculum Key Stages 1 and 2 (2007) *Thinking Skills and Personal Capabilities: CPD Materials*. www.nicurriculum.org/key stages_1 and_2.
49. Dowling, M. (2005) *Supporting Young Children's Sustained Shared Thinking: An exploration*. London: Early Education.
50. Dowling, M. (2008) *Exploring Young Children's Thinking through their Self-chosen Activities*. London: Early Education.
51. Piaget, J. (1968) *Six Psychological Studies*. London: University of London Press.
52. Piaget, J. (1953) *The Origins of Intelligence in Children*. London: Routledge and Kegan Paul.
53. Athey, C. (2007) *Extending Thought in Young Children* (2nd edn). London: Paul Chapman.
54. Bruner, J. (1966) *Towards a Theory of Instruction*. New York: W.W. Norton.
55. Robson (2006) *Developing Thinking and Understanding in Young Children* (see note 8), p. 118.

2

Early Thoughts: Babies' and Infants' Thinking from Birth to Three Years

Intentions

This chapter:

- recognises the capability of babies and infants to think
- considers the very young child's primary need for a close attachment
- understands how the very young child:
  - becomes a thinking person in his own right and starts to understand the minds of others
  - thinks flexibly, makes sense of experiences, imagines and communicates his thoughts and ideas

There has been a revolution in our understanding of babies. We now know that they are far more competent and capable than we ever realised. No longer do we regard young babies as helpless but, as Maria Robinson describes, 'a brain in waiting' (1). We see the baby from the start of life using all the equipment in his small body and brain to make sense of this new world into which he has arrived.

> Babies do not need to be taught how to think. They are born with mental abilities that fully function to allow them to make sense of experiences and anticipate future events. (2)

The receptive young brain

The nature/nurture question has taxed us for many years, that is, which is most important – our genetic features or the environment in which we are raised? We now recognise that while every child is born with a body and brain, it is what happens from then on that determines how that baby develops. From the word 'go', babies are interested in their world and particularly the people who are close to them. From birth the baby can already recognise his mother's voice and rapidly becomes sensitised to her smell. He is attracted to faces and very soon is able to recognise his mum and dad's faces when held in their arms. He is equipped to reach out to the world and it is these experiences that affect the ways in which his brain grows and develops.

When a baby is exposed to experiences again and again the delicate threads which link or connect brain cells are strengthened through use. Using these connectors, the baby starts to make sense of all that is happening around him. All experiences will have some impact on the baby's brain, but it is the consistent and repetitive experiences that will nourish the connectors and make them grow strong. Eventually, these strong connectors establish patterns of learning. The fine threads or connectors which are not fed with experiences will eventually wither away through lack of use. The old maxim *use it or lose it* applies. And because the young brain is so receptive, this highlights the importance of providing these nourishing experiences during the earliest months of life.

Two years later an active toddler is reaching out to explore the world. Manning Morton suggests that most two year olds approach life as if it were a major research project (3). They are fascinated by things and people and closely observe the ways of the world. Their increased mobility means that they can move freely to investigate and come into contact with more people and objects. They also explore through using other senses, listening, observing, smelling and touching.

Feeling close, loved and secure

In her wonderful book *Why Love Matters*, Sue Gerhardt points out that young brains are strengthened through warm and loving relationships and this starts in the home (4). The baby has been physically attached to his mum in the womb and when he pops out he simply won't survive if set adrift. The baby desperately seeks protection from the person who is closest to him. Nowadays we have developed and extended this interpretation of simple physical need and recognise that love is fundamental for all aspects of a young child's development (and indeed our own), but is particularly important at the start of life.

'Attachment' is the term given to the special nature of a relationship that is very close. It is to do with feeling understood, knowing that we matter to someone and that someone will meet our needs. It can be summed up by feeling close, safe and loved. An initial sound attachment is like an inoculation against the stresses and knocks that young children come up against later in life.

The deepest part of the brain is concerned with feelings and its development is fundamental to all other aspects of development. From a safe and secure base the young baby will start to explore her environment and become open to new experiences.

And so if a baby is securely wrapped in a mantle of love, he will feel relaxed and comfortable and will be able to take note of and respond to the world around him. This comfortable state occurs because the baby's stress is managed for him by his special person; it is reflected by low levels of the stress hormone cortisol in his body. However, cortisol levels can rocket if the baby feels abandoned and alone. Without the support of a strong attachment, babies will vary in their response: some will be highly sensitive to the slightest stress, showing tension and producing a lot of cortisol; at the other end of the spectrum babies can start to repress their feelings and appear passive and disinterested, which causes their cortisol levels to be depressed. Both high levels of stress and repressed stress powerfully inhibit a person's inclination and ability to explore new things and ideas, and babies are no exception.

Above all else, then, a baby needs a strong and secure attachment with at least one special person and this serves as the bedrock for his future learning and thinking. He will also become close to other family members, including siblings, and when he moves to a group setting with a key person or when a childminder becomes his key person.

Social understandings

Being separate and distinct

As a result of experiences of being secure and cared for, a baby becomes confident and strengthens his identity. Around nine months he is busy discovering new things but now recognises that his concerns may be shared by others. He will track an object that someone else is involved with and will alert another person to something of interest by pointing to it. This indicates that the baby begins to understand that he is a person in his own right, that other people are separate from him with their own thoughts and feelings but that they may share his interest. It is called a 'theory of mind'. Not only does he use pointing to draw his close person's attention to something, he may also use her as a social reference. The baby looks to his close person to see how she is responding to something new – a stranger coming into the room, a sudden shower of rain, a new piece of equipment. The baby is still heavily influenced by his special person and will tend to imitate her reactions to a situation.

By responding promptly and sensitively to the baby's signals, the adult is helping him to understand how he can gain her attention and enjoy these early moments of shared thinking.

Becoming aware of others' viewpoints, feelings and intentions

Although a new baby is amazingly competent, he is not born with a social brain. He is totally dependent on his experiences with those close to him which re-enforces yet again the importance of a good attachment. We know from Margaret Donaldson's influential work that when young children are in everyday situations that make sense to them, they show to best effect the power of their thinking (5). The most familiar context for most babies and toddlers is in the home (for some, of course, it is in the home of a childminder or in group settings with a key person). There have been no conclusive studies about how very young children develop in group settings but Judy Dunn has shown that even babies in their first year are sensitive to those who are close to them and start to understand that their family members have minds that are different from their own. Toddlers less than two years old show some understanding of how older siblings will react when teased or annoyed (6). They observe and are able to 'tune in' to quarrels between members of their family. Their behaviour is sympathetic and supportive to the member of the family who is upset, but they also recognise and enjoy joining in with a joke.

Dunn's work offers powerful evidence of how, even before they can talk, very young children take a real interest in and begin to understand how other people behave. As yet they are not able to appreciate another's perspective in an intellectual task, but already they work from a sharp social intelligence and can make out others' emotions. The ability to empathise – to tune into the feelings of others – is heavily dependent on a young child having her own feelings understood. Once children can talk, they show further signs of understanding others' minds. By three years, children in another of Dunn's studies were able to recognise, anticipate and respond to the feelings of their baby brothers or sisters (7).

Babies also progress from being able to copy a person to beginning to understand what that person intends. Amazingly, newborn babies can imitate the facial expressions of others close to them, which imply that they are already starting to link what they see with how the other person is feeling.

There are now tentative findings indicating that by seven months the baby starts to understand that a person's actions are intentional. One method to determine this is by using 'looking time', which relies on the fact that babies look longer at unexpected events than expected ones. In one such study, two of the baby's toys – say a doll and a ball – are placed on a table. A person's hand reaches out and grabs the ball. Then the position of the toys is switched so that the ball is now where the doll was. When the hand reaches out this time for the doll, the baby looks longer at this choice, predicting that she would have reached for the ball even though its position is changed. Interestingly, the babies who were able to do this were those who could reach for objects themselves, which suggests that their own experiences help them to understand the intentions of others (8).

The world of possibilities

The parts of the young brain that deal with feelings are in place at birth, while the pre-frontal cortex, which is to do with thinking, planning and focusing, develops much later and grows slowly; it is only fully developed in adults. It might be thought that as babies lack these mature, adult structures they are wanting, but current research argues that this lack can actually be a benefit (9, 10). The pre-frontal cortex assists thinking as it helps us to restrict distractions, narrow our options and allows the thinker to concentrate on the topic. It inhibits a person from becoming bogged down by all sorts of alternatives. Babies and toddlers lack this inhibitor but instead are open to all possibilities. A walk with a toddler can prove a frustrating or intriguing experience, depending on the time you have and the frame of mind you are in. If you need to get to the shops quickly, your toddler's exploration on the journey of every paving stone, mini beast and stone in the gutter can exasperate; however, if you can join your child in his investigation, the world can become a different place as you share his wonder in the mundane.

Gopnik suggests that because babies can't yet focus on anything particular they are able to be more flexible. Their options are endless. Older babies, like adults, are strongly attracted to new or unexpected events and, just like adults, they also lose attention when they get bored. However, the difference is that while adults can be interested in both general external events and also in something of particular interest and relevance to them, babies are entranced by everything and anything. This initial ability to hoover up so much information provides babies and infants with a fund of rich experiences (11).

Thinking away from the here and now

We used to think that babies' minds were firmly rooted in the present. However, predictable and loving routines allow them to recognise a signal and anticipate an event.

Case Study 2.1

Eight month old Anitha, exploring a treasure basket, suddenly stopped. She had heard the sound of a key turn in the door outside. Anitha's eyes widened and a broad smile spread on her face. There were sounds of footsteps outside the door and Anitha watched as the doorknob to the living room slowly turned. She squealed with anticipation and stretched out her arms as her daddy's face appeared around the door.

Comment

Anitha had grown used to these daily, familiar signals which allowed her to connect them with her dad's arrival and his loving greeting. She used her powers of prediction, awaiting this important moment.

Gopnik's studies also suggest that in certain situation these very young children can also envisage possibilities for the future. One test she carried out was to see if a baby could consider possibilities for a task and select the best option. Babies were given a post with stacking rings to place on it, but one of the rings had the hole taped over. At 15 months, babies attempted to solve the problem by forcing the ring on to the post, trying again and eventually giving up. Three months later at 18 months, babies stacked the rings but refused even to try to fit the taped ring – they appeared to understand what would happen if they did and that it was a lost cause. While the younger babies used trial and error to complete the task, the older babies didn't need to check if the taped ring would fit, but seemed able to imagine the consequences.

Young three year olds are also able to think about the possibilities of an alternative past. When told a story about a duck with muddy shoes who had walked into a kitchen, they recognised the consequence that the floor would be dirty. However, when questioned about what would happen if the duck had cleaned his boots first, the children surmised that the floor would be clean (12).

Both of these examples demonstrate very young children's ability to think counterfactually, that is to imagine a situation and consider the consequences of a situation that is different from the one before them. Given a scenario that they can understand, they are able to reach back into past events and project forward. This early flexible thinking is the precursor to older children's ability to identify and solve problems, reflecting on what might be rather than what is.

Object/person permanence

A further leap in thinking occurs when babies start to understand that something they can see no longer still exists. Before this, a baby under eight or nine months believes that when an article or person disappears from sight it is gone for ever. Kwame, at eight months, was playing with a soft toy monkey. He handed it to his dad and appeared to watch as dad hid the monkey under the sofa. Kwame behaved as if the monkey no longer existed, even when dad reached under the sofa to retrieve it. Thinking in the present, the baby believes that if you can't see it, it's not there. Around nine or ten months, the baby takes a mental step forward. He learns that an article can be hidden and retrieved and enjoys practising this game for himself, testing that the object can always be rediscovered. This understanding of the permanence of objects extends to person permanence and is closely linked to a baby's readiness to be separated from his special person. Initially, a young baby is not unduly upset if mum disappears and he is given into the care of a friendly but unfamiliar person. Once mum departs, he appears no longer to keep her in his mind. However, the older baby is more knowledgeable. He understands that mum's disappearance does not mean that she has gone for ever. He can still hold her in his mind and remember her. He grasps the possibility of her continued presence somewhere and he becomes anxious and fretful to have her back.

Making sense

Discovering the world through moving and sensing

Early motor and sensory experiences allow babies and infants to absorb, sort out and make sense of the world around them. All five senses – taste, smell, sound, sight and touch – are used in the child's exploration, but sight and sound emerge early on and need to be stimulated in order for the child to develop normally.

Margaret Donaldson described movement as thought in action:

> Children have first to experience the world actively through all their senses before they can think in the abstract and hold thoughts on the memory of those things in their heads as pictures, concepts or symbols. (13)

The brain and body work together through the physical senses. Babies and infants will initially find out about the people and things around them through physical experiences and express their thoughts and feelings through movement, sound and gestures. They are growing to understand the world using enactive representations to make sense, as suggested by Bruner (14).

At six months babies are more mobile and can grab their feet. The baby's brain links with his sense of touch and he starts to recognise the parts of his body that are his feet. Babies become aware of more parts of their bodies by around 13 months, at the same time that they recognise themselves in a mirror. They also become aware of the spaces where their body is located, which makes it important to keep the layout of an environment familiar. Balance is the first of the sensory systems to mature and is the basis for the development of co-ordination, stable eye movements and visual perception. Mobile infants learn about securing their body to the ground and keeping a balance through movement and touch – they experience how to balance their body differently as they stagger across grassy, stony and or a soft, sand surface or use a rail or sofa to steady themselves when climbing up a step or moving around a corner. These rich and varied experiences conveyed through movement, give infants more and more information about the world in which they live. As they revisit these experiences again and again, they begin to piece them together and come to conclusions. Over time they begin to recall how their feet sink into a sandpit or how they use their feet and legs to push their bodies up the step. These memories are the start of thinking in the abstract, described by Donaldson (15).

Early schema

We have seen how fundamental movement is to support thinking and a baby's attention does become more selective as he becomes preoccupied by certain patterns of action. There is a fascinating dichotomy in that babies are concerned with making lots of connections and learning as much as they can as early as possible; however, they also refine these connections and start to concentrate on the ones which interest them most.

Piaget aptly described babies and young children as little scientists (16); one aspect of this is their need to repeat actions such as dropping and throwing things or transporting objects from one place to another. Babies discover, seemingly quite by accident, that they can make items fall to the floor or move. They repeat this action again and again, and so methodically test out that their actions result in a predictable response. Over time babies become particularly interested and familiar with certain actions or patterns of movement and will try them out in different situations. A baby may be absorbed placing large beads from a box into a bag – when she becomes mobile she extends this interest in transporting by piling blocks into a buggy and taking them to the role-play area. These repeated patterns of behaviour are called schema. Chris Athey's Froebel study of young children's thinking used Piaget's description of the four different levels of schema operations. These are:

- **Level one:** sensorimotor level, where children use their senses, action and movement to play out their interests.
- **Level two:** symbolic level, where children understand that one thing can be used to represent something else.

- **Level three**: functional dependency level, where children begin to understand cause and effect.
- **Level four**: abstract thought level, where children describe what they are doing through talk (17).

Babies and infants will most likely demonstrate their schematic thinking at levels one and two.

Some of the common and absorbing types of schema that can engross very young children are:

- **Positioning**: lining up play objects or placing them in groups, e.g. positioning blocks and small world people and vehicles.
- **Enveloping**: covering themselves or objects, e.g. covering themselves in a sheet, placing objects into containers, wrapping things up.
- **Enclosing**: placing boundaries around objects, e.g. placing a fence around animals in a field.
- **Transporting**: carrying objects from one place to another, e.g. using a pushchair to move blocks from the block area to the role-play area.
- **Rotating**: turning/spinning themselves or objects, e.g. running around in circles outside, using ribbon sticks and streamers for making circular movements in the air.
- **Trajectory**: creating lines in space, e.g. jumping in the air, dropping things from a height.

Children often have a very strong drive to repeat actions, such as moving things from one place to another, covering things up and putting things into containers, or moving in circles or throwing things. These patterns can often be observed running through their play and may vary between one child and another. If practitioners build on these interests, powerful learning can take place (18).

Case Study 2.2

Claudine, at ten months old, has already had many opportunities to handle materials, reach, select and explore items from treasure baskets. When moving on to heuristic play, this toddler develops a particular interest in enclosures – ordering, combining and placing items in enclosed spaces. ... She selects a necklace and repeatedly returns to attempt to fix it around her neck. Moving on, she find wooden pegs and spends a great deal of time fixing them in a circular pattern around a wooden container. She spends time dropping necklaces into boxes and fixing on the lid. Later in

(Continued)

(Continued)

her play Claudine encloses herself in a space behind the sofa – she has created her den.

Comment

During this episode of play Claudine has drawn from her plentiful experiences investigating items, and in heuristic play she is starting to think about what items are for and how they can be used. Claudine has become very focused on enclosing things and herself in spaces. This strand of thought may fade away as she develops other interests, but equally it might persist in other contexts. Claudine may later deepen her preoccupation with enclosing when building structures or when drawing a border around her paintings. She may make links with other schema as she extends her interests.

Stella Louis describes other ways in which children's actions reveal an interest in creating enclosed spaces.

> Young children are sometimes observed building 'Bridging Enclosures' as they begin to make connections between different structures and enclosures. They may make other enclosures with straight and angled lines. Most children who make enclosures fill them in an ordered way. The enclosure schema has close ties with trajectory, connecting, enveloping and positioning schemas and practitioners may often observe behaviour combined with other schemas (19).

Making and marking

Babies and infants are also very flexible in the ways they represent their thoughts and ideas. They will use anything that is available. Marian Whitehead suggests that one of the earliest examples of making meaning is during the earliest months of life:

> most noticeably when the infant endows a soft toy or blanket ... with a wealth of feeling and significance – so much so that comfort in stressful situations or in the minutes before falling asleep appear to depend on it utterly. This drive continues as children cuddle and talk to objects and toys, pretend to be things and try to interpret the marks they notice in their world. These behaviours are clearly reflections of children's ability to make meaning out of arbitrary signs. (20)

Kate Pahl's study of nursery-age children making meaning endorses this view as it shows young children using a range of stuff available to them to make stories, including drawing and representing through cutting out and model making (21).

Common observations in settings support this and show how two and three year olds 'replay' their understandings using malleable materials, dough and clay, building with blocks and sticking and making. Using all these resources they create and transform meanings naturally and easily.

Making marks is also a central way of them fixing their experiences in time, although babies and infants initially just make marks for the sheer pleasure of doing so. As soon as she can sit independently, a baby will start to make marks. At this stage she will simply enjoy the physical experience of making patterns in her food or making interesting marks with jam or chocolate on her body. Given a pen, pencil or chalk, she will make lots of random marks on any available surface – walls, floors and paper. These experiences lead very young children to recognise that they can actually make a mark and produce an effect. Mark making is no longer random but becomes intentional. Matthews states that very young children develop their mark making skills using whatever comes to hand. He suggests that they represent movement, feelings and thoughts visually through:

- figures, suggesting the shape of an object
- action, using the mark maker to convey movement in time and space, e.g. rapid circular movement which can appear as 'scribble' may depict *me in a fast car* (22).

Drawing and painting are only one form of representation. When infants draw, paint and combine this with making and doing, their learning is multi-modal and very strong as they combine their actions with what they are thinking and feeling (23). These representations offer us further insights into the child's mind.

Eventually the infant begins to understand that marks are symbols and can stand for other things. The young child's marks become her own personal symbols. A mature three year old starts to distinguish between drawing and writing and will 'read' you the messages conveyed in her mark making.

Making sense of second-hand experiences

Although we know that first-hand experiences are the most valuable for very young children, exposure to books and pictures also play a very important role. The reality is also that they are increasingly exposed to screen media. If we accept this somewhat unpalatable fact, we find that studies show infants to be critical viewers, often deciding what they want to watch, showing when they are bored and attending with interest to certain programmes (24). Watching a screen is certainly not a passive activity but involves intricate, cognitive processes. Infants are required to translate a 2-D representation into a 3-D object, and at the same time connect what they are viewing to their real-life experiences. It is no surprise, then, that infants find it much more difficult to understand and make sense of video footage rather than real things. However, screen viewing planned with care can help to widen their knowledge of the world, giving them information that they cannot gain first-hand. And they accumulate this knowledge in their remarkable minds.

By six months, babies can take on board material from DVD/TV, store it in their memories and use this later in early imitation. By 12 months, infants can distinguish different categories of items which look similar. For example, given two almost identical plastic toys of a plane and bird with outstretched wings, they will make them move in very different ways. Exposure to screen media showing different types of flight can help this concept development, which many infants will not be able to experience directly (25). One small-scale study which considered the responses of two year old children to the programme *Teletubbies* provides some positive messages. The children responded to the simple questions posed and appeared to make sense of the rituals of bed-time and hide and seek. Above all, they enjoyed immensely seeing familiar characters, recognising the tricks played and joining in with the music and rhythm (26).

Despite these upbeat examples, there remains the question about whether exposure to screen viewing is really beneficial for such very young children. Many experts have reservations and oppose findings which suggest positive gains. Aric Sigman points to studies which suggest a link between viewing television and attention deficit (27). Sigman quotes a study of 1–3 year olds which found that even background television reduced the length and quality of their play (28). David Elkind reserves judgement, believing that it is too early to judge the effect of heavy visual stimulation on the other senses (29).

The jury is still out on the relative merits and dangers of introducing screen-based learning to babies and infants and selective evidence (much of which relates to older children) can be used to support either view. However, very young children are particularly vulnerable. While recognising that occasional selected programmes may offer useful experiences, we should be extremely cautious about the amount of time that is allocated to viewing. Above all we should emphasise the need for adult companionship to tune into and support the very young child's meaning making.

Creating imaginary worlds

The Tickell Review of the Early Years Foundation Stage identifies 'Creating and Thinking Critically' as one of the enduring characteristics of learning. It involves young children:

- having their own ideas [being ingenious in approaching and trying to solve problems]

- using what they already know to learn new things [making a connection between experiences – putting two and two together]
- choosing to do things and finding new ways [planning, managing and sometimes adapting their thinking, being intentional]. (30)

All aspects of this characteristic are visible in very young children, although sometimes at an embryonic stage. However, imaginative play has an important role. It offers babies and infants great opportunities to use their experiences, muse around with ideas, try things out and be open to all sorts of possibilities.

Babies in their first year learn fast through imitation. At first, the sensitive close person will imitate the baby's facial gestures and body movements and this reciprocity builds a pattern of close communication which affirms the baby's actions and helps her to start to understand other people and what they do. Babies watch closely the daily and increasingly predictable actions of those around them, and by the end of his first year a young child is keen to apparently copy actions that he has observed, using a mobile phone or sweeping the floor. But David and co-authors suggest that this apparent copying is actually a reconstruction – the child's own version of what she has observed and noted and then transformed (31). As the older baby begins to recognise that the objects are permanent and develops understanding of a 'theory of mind', the ability to pretend emerges. Tina Bruce suggests that toddlers start to rehearse roles, pretend and create play props as they become able to imagine and play with symbols. 'Children at play are able to stay flexible, respond to events and changing situations, be sensitive to people, to adapt, think on their feet and keep altering what they do in a fast moving scene' (32).

When an infant begins to recognise that one thing stands for another, he has moved forward in his thinking. Around 14 months, the infant may do this with objects that have something in common – she may wrap her teddy in a newspaper if a blanket is not available. Later, she extends her use of symbols and make-believes that anything is possible – the space behind the sofa can become a post box and a cardboard box may be turned into a boat, house or plane, all within the space of a few minutes. This power of effortless transformation allows the toddler to have some control over her world. Through pretend play, very young children are beginning to use symbols, form images or imagine things that are not present or may not even exist. And we now know that babies can pretend before they can talk, although once they use language they have a powerful way of putting their ideas together. Pretend play is the beginning of abstract thought. By around the age of two, children spend much of their time in a world of imaginary possibilities, but Gopnik states that they know that they are pretending and can distinguish between the actual and fictitious world (33).

We have always recognised that young children live in the world of pretend for much of the time, and formerly we took this as a sign of them being unable to distinguish between real life and make-believe. Now we know that even toddlers, if they wish to, are able to separate the two; this is evident from their giggles if you try to participate in their play – around three years, some children will ask you to join in and then tell you clearly if you are not playing in accordance with their plan. If you try hard to be realistic in your role, children can even become concerned for you and make it clear that 'it's not real, you know – only pretend'!

Two and three year old children are incredibly imaginative – their minds roam into far-flung places. They are not inhibited by a developed pre-frontal cortex nor are their feet chained to the ground by 'common sense'. They simply give free rein to their impulses, being open to any alternatives; what they don't know they make up and this makes their thoughts and ideas wonderfully individual. And this is most visible when very young children play. At these times we can witness their imaginative thoughts and ideas in action. As Hope suggests, this is a profound foundation for later development:

> Playing with ideas is not just the highest form of intellectual activity, it is also the most fundamental. It is where we all begin: to wonder, to think and to become independent rational beings (34).

Case Study 2.3

Fourteen month old Chloe was fascinated with mark making. She also enjoyed visiting the post box with her mum and helping to post letters into the box. At home she sat with her granddad and made marks with him. Later that day Chloe laboriously posted her 'letters' underneath the door in the downstairs shower room. She was delighted when granddad joined in the play and posted back some letters to Chloe through the crack in the kitchen door.

Comment

Chloe's play represents her interests and understanding. At this stage, Chloe is perfectly happy to accept that anything could 'become' a post box. One year later, she was more selective and chose to use a cardboard box which she had helped her mum convert into a familiar red pillar box. She moved on to elaborate her play by carefully pushing her letters into envelopes and making a mark for a stamp.

Communicating through behaviour and language

Communication and language is closely linked to the development of thought. The ability of the very young child to make meaning from what they know of the world and to extend their understandings is heavily influenced by their growing command of spoken language (35). A report commissioned by the government and based on data from a large, longitudinal study examined the early communication environment for children in their first two years. The findings confirm research conclusions from a number of smaller studies and include the unequivocal statement that language development at the age of two years predicts children's performance on entry to primary school (36). However, as we have seen earlier in this chapter, babies are already thinking before they can talk (37).

A baby's and infant's preoccupations or schema also provide us with valuable information about what is going on in their minds. We know very well when the very young child is interested and absorbed in something by his focused attention and repeated patterns of behaviour. He communicates through movement and facial expression. A baby's pleasure is evident when he wriggles his body in anticipation or beams when his close adult touches him lovingly. When he is tired, the baby may switch off, turn away from contacts or simply grizzle. Frustrations are made equally clear through bursts of angry crying. Before children use spoken language we are dependent on tuning into their interests and responses by observing their levels of concentration, eye gaze, facial expressions, body language and gestures. These non-verbal languages provide very important insights into the thoughts of very young children and should be taken seriously.

Around 9–12 months the signs of spoken language develop with babies babbling and using personal sounds to express their needs and requests. First words emerge around 12 months and these one- and two-word utterances are often shorthand for full sentences. The beginning of verbal thinking is described by Whitehead as having two characteristics: the very young child's curiosity about words and a rapid increase in her vocabulary. She also refers to the stage when infants talk to themselves when playing and suggests that this self-talk is possibly a link between the development of talk and talk for thinking (38). We see in Chapter 4 how self-talk is a signal of self-regulated and intentional behaviour.

Practical Activity

Listen to your key children regularly and frequently and note:

- when they use language to begin to self-regulate their actions, for example, when standing by the edge of a pond to feed the ducks and reminding themselves to beware of falling in – *steady, steady.*
- examples of grammatical errors that show the child's growing understanding of grammatical rules, for example, shoeses, mices.

Sally Goddard Blythe suggests that music and social engagement are the early foundations of communication and that babies and infants have a special language which is more like music and mime than speech. Blythe quotes Charles Darwin, who in 1872 wrote: 'I have been led to infer that the progenitors of man probably uttered musical tones before they had acquired the powers of articulate speech' (39).

Meaningful musical exchanges can take place within the first few weeks of life. Trevarthen's research shows us that when a mother is closely attuned to her baby, a musical conversation occurs. The mum sings a short musical phrase to her baby and, if she waits, the baby sings a response. This conversation showed all the features of musical composition. Importantly, though, if the adult didn't give the baby time to reply, the baby gave up and the dialogue ended (40).

Infants have a growing command of words but often it is not sufficient to express their needs. A two year old's temper tantrums often arise because his physical skills are not yet sufficient to carry out his intentions and yet he cannot convey this fluently through talk.

A strong spirit of enquiry is evident in early communication. Babies seek to find out initially by pointing to an object that interests them. Around 17 months, an infant may name things in a questioning way. 'Doggie' may simply be a descriptive statement but also implies a question: 'Is it a dog?' A two year old will start to use questioning words, such as 'what?', 'who?', 'where?' and the incessant 'why?'. Infants also seek to make sense of information by grouping or categorising things into types. Many two year olds are intensely interested in insects. They group these together and everything that crawls or flies becomes a 'flug'. Again, they may seek affirmation from the adult by pointing and using 'flug' as a question, meaning 'Am I right – is this a "flug"?' The drive to know fuels early talk. Above all, communication and language develops by doing things with other people. This is discussed in the next chapter.

Main messages in this chapter

- Babies are born with a huge interest and intent to reach out and make sense of the world: their thinking capacities are strengthened through warm and loving relationships.
- Around nine months, babies begin to recognise themselves as separate and distinct from others as they develop a 'theory of mind' and can understand that objects and people still exist even though they disappear from sight.
- In familiar contexts they learn to imitate those close to them and start to be aware of the feelings and intentions of others.
- Their early flexible thinking allows them to consider a range of possibilities, this being a requirement for later problem solving.

- Their thinking strengthens as they move and use other senses, explore and connect particular interests or schema, imagine, reconstruct what they have observed and noted, and start to represent their experiences through symbols.
- They develop imaginative thoughts and ideas in play which are the precursors to abstract thought.
- Babies and infants relay their thoughts and ideas initially through their behaviour and body gestures and then through words, including self-talk to direct their thoughts and actions.

References

1. Robinson, M. (2009) *The Wonder Year: 1st Year Development and Shaping the Brain*. Siren Films Ltd, www.sirenfilms.co.uk.
2. Gopnik, A., Meltzoff, A. and Kuhl, P. (1999) *How Babies Think*. London: Weidenfield and Nicolson, p. 271.
3. Manning Morton, J. (2005) 'Working with Two-Year-Olds', *Nursery World*, 5 May, p. 23.
4. Gerhardt, S. (2004) *Why Love Matters*. London: Brunner-Routledge.
5. Donaldson, M. (1978) *Children's Minds*. London: Fontana.
6. Dunn, J. and Kendrick, C. (1982) *Siblings: Love, Envy and Understanding*. Cambridge, MA: Harvard University Press.
7. Dunn, J. (1999) 'Mindreading and Social Relationships', in M. Bennett (ed.), *Developmental Psychology*. London: Taylor & Francis, pp. 55–71.
8. Gopnik, A. and Seiver, E. (2009) 'Reading Minds', *Birth to Three*, 28 November, p. 2.
9. Gopnik, A. (2009) *The Philosophical Baby*. London: Bodley Head.
10. Scott, B.K. (2010) 'The Magic of Pre-School', *Psychology Today*, 28 July.
11. Gopnik (2009) *The Philosophical Baby* (see note 9), pp. 118, 119.
12. Ibid., pp. 24, 26.
13. Donaldson (1978) *Children's Minds* (see note 5), p. 37.
14. Bruner, J. (1966) *Towards a Theory of Instruction*. New York: W.W. Norton.
15. Donaldson (1978) *Children's Minds* (see note 5), p.76.
16. Piaget, J. (1950) *The Psychology of Intelligence*. London: Routledge and Kegan Paul.
17. Athey, C. (2007) *Extending Thought in Young Children* (2nd edn). London: Paul Chapman, p. 131.
18. www.standards.dfes.gov.uk/eyfs/site/glossary/index.htm.
19. Louis, S., Beswick, C., Magraw, L. and Hayes, L. (2009) in S. Featherstone (ed.) *Again! Again!* London: A & C Black, p. 49.
20. Whitehead, M. (2004) *Language and Literacy in the Early Years*. London: Sage, p. 172.
21. Pahl, K. (1999) *Transformations: Children's Meaning Making in a Nursery*. Stoke on Trent: Trentham Books.
22. Matthews, J. (1999) *The Art of Childhood and Adolescence: The Construction of Meaning*. London: Falmer Press.

23. Kress, G. (1997) *Rethinking the Paths to Literacy*. London: Routledge.
24. Karmiloff, K. and Karmilff-Smith, A. (2011) 'TV Times', *Nursery World*, 17 February, p. 22.
25. Ibid., p. 23.
26. Roberts, S. and Howard, S. (2005) 'Watching Teletubbies: Television and its Very Young Audience', in J. Marsh (ed.), *Popular Culture, New Media and Digital Literacy in Early Childhood*. London: Routledge/Falmer, pp. 91–107.
27. Sigman, A. (2007) *Remotely Controlled: How TV is Damaging Our Lives*. London: Vermillion.
28. Sigman, A. (2011) 'Does Not Compute, Revisited: Screen Technology in Early Years Education', in R. House (ed.), *Too Much, Too Soon*. London: Hawthorn Press, p. 269.
29. Elkind, D. (2007) *The Hurried Child: Growing Up Too Fast Too Soon* (3rd edn). Cambridge, MA: Da Capo Press.
30. Tickell, C. (2011) *The Early Years: Foundations for Life, Health and Learning*. An Independent Report to HM Government on the Early Years Foundation Stage. London: Department for Education, p. 90.
31. David, T., Gooch, K., Powell, S. and Abbott, A. (2003) *Birth to Three Matters: A Review of the Literature*. Research Report 444. London: Department for Education and Skills.
32. Bruce, T. (2001) *Learning through Play: Babies, Toddlers and the Foundation Years*. London: Hodder Arnold, p. 46.
33. Gopnik (2009) *The Philosophical Baby* (see note 9), p. 30.
34. Hope, G. (2008) *Thinking and Learning through Drawing*. London: Sage, p. 17.
35. Vygotsky, L.S. (1978) *Mind in Society*. Cambridge, MA: Harvard University Press.
36. Roulstone, S., Law, J., Rush, R., Clegg, J. and Peters, T. (2011) *Investigating the Role of Language in Children's Early Educational Outcomes*. Research Report 134. London: Department for Education.
37. Mandler, J. (1999) 'Preverbal Representation and Language', in P. Bloom, M. Peterson, L. Nadel and M. Garsett (eds), *Language and Space*. Cambridge MA: MIT Press, pp. 365–84.
38. Whitehead (2004) *Language and Literacy in the Early Years* (see note 20), pp. 76, 77.
39. Goddard Blythe, S. (2009) 'All about Movement and Music', *Nursery World*, 3 December, p. 17.
40. Trevarthen, C. (2006) 'Pleasure from Others' Movements: How Body Massage and Music Speak with One Voice to Infants and Give Meaning to Life'. Paper presented at the Guild of Infant and Child Massage (GICM) Conference, Coventry, October.

How Close Adults can Support Babies' and Infants' Thinking

Intentions

This chapter:

- recognises the central role of the parent and special person in ensuring that the baby and infant feels secure, loved and cared for
- considers how close adults:
  - offer companionship, supporting the very young child's growing abilities to communicate thoughts and ideas
  - support the child's transition from home
  - provide opportunities for movement, sensory experiences and representations of what the very young child has encountered
  - promote early intentions by encouraging early independence and allowing time for thought processes to emerge and develop

Once our eyes are opened to the powerful tools that very young children use to make sense of their world we become acutely aware of the need to provide the best conditions for these tools to operate. The most important resources are the adult and the relationships that are developed, and then the climate or environment that supports and provokes early thoughts.

Relationships

Attachment and attunement

Babies and young children cannot become competent learners and thinkers until they feel secure, loved and cared for by a person (or persons) who becomes special to them. The most powerful attachments are based on contingent care where the special person is closely tuned in to the baby's signals – his facial expressions, body movements and sounds. Not only can she read these signals, but the special person will respond in a way which is specially designed to meet the baby's needs.

Maria Robinson describes attunement as:

> not only an understanding of the baby's signals, it is an overall acceptance of who the baby is – the individual temperament, pace and rhythm of this particular child. The parent is able to accommodate and adjust their own temperament, pace and rhythm to that of the child, allowing the child room to be itself while learning about the mother and in turn learning about itself. (1)

Parents who have lived with their babies from birth are in a prime position to offer attuned and bespoke responses to their baby. However there may be teething problems. Parents share the joy and exhilaration of growing the baby, the anticipation and experience of the birth. Then follow the pleasures, but also the never-ending responsibilities of caring for a young baby, and the fatigue that follows. The reality of living for and caring for this tiny, new and dependent person can be very daunting for a new parent. But, given the right conditions at home, young and first-time parents will grow in confidence by learning the mechanics of caring for the baby and then growing to recognise and understand the signals of this unique individual who needs them so much and who they quickly recognise as being indispensable to them.

Becoming attuned

Attunement is a natural extension of attachment. Through becoming close and loving, the special person becomes familiar with the baby. Attunement means being on the same wavelength as the baby, which is sometimes described as a 'dance of dialogue' (2). The most important aspect of this 'dance' is that it is tailor-made or bespoke to that particular baby.

Become familiar with the child's unique characteristics

- What interests her and how long can she sustain this interest?
- How does she show she is tired or uncomfortable?
- What do her signals and gestures convey?

The special person will show that she recognises the baby's signals and, through smiles, gestures and warm touch, will respond to her needs.

Using 'parentese'
Most babies love musical sounds and the key person will bring in interest to a 'conversation' through using songs and rhymes. She will also

talk to the baby almost instinctively, adapting her voice and facial expressions to make messages clear. This way of speaking and looking is described as 'parentese' and involves:

- slowing down the voice and speaking in a musical way
- exaggerating the vowel sounds
- using facial expressions that are larger than life move close to the baby, raising eyebrows and smiling widely.

Use of 'parentese' is an invitation for the baby to 'catch' and copy the messages, which in turn invite another response from the special person. Repeated dialogues or conversations with babies during their earliest months of life provide them with a strong social foundation of security and a basis for moving towards further stimulus. Robinson goes further and suggests that through these intimate 'conversations' the parent is behaving towards the baby as if he is a person in his own right (3).

Nurturing development

Babies and infants also need to be stimulated and challenged, and findings from the Effective Provision of Pre-School Education Project suggest that what parents and carers do with their children during the first three years makes a real difference to development. The project highlights specific activities that can be helpful:

- reading to children
- teaching children songs and nursery rhymes
- playing with letters and numbers
- painting and drawing
- taking children to libraries
- creating regular opportunities for play with friends (4).

This involves providing new stimulus for babies and infants, introducing them to symbols and providing them with opportunities to mix with their peers, observe and play alongside them and start to exchange ideas.

Although these messages are a helpful steer for parents, they should be aware that the effect of these activities with such very young children is heavily dependent on their age and stage of development. For example, a one year old may enjoy a visit to a library simply to toddle around book boxes, explore spaces and share one or two picture books with a special person. Parents need to be alert to when their child is ready to respond to new stimulus and how it is introduced. In addition, the impact on young babies and infants will be more powerful if they are linked to some of the principles of companionable learning outlined in Chapter 1 (5). For instance, children at this age will:

- respond more readily to stories, songs and library visits if they can secure the time, attention and loving encouragement from their parent (companionable attention)
- be fascinated and take pleasure in the company of other babies and infants but only if they already have a sound attachment with their parent and can view others from that secure base (companionable attention)
- enjoy playing with symbols and mark making if this is offered in the spirit of shared play and only when parents recognise that their child is interested (companionable play).

Questions when working with parents

How well do I help parents to recognise the significance of secure attachment for their baby's well-being and development?

From this sensitive beginning of understanding the individual needs of the baby, there is also born the beginnings for the baby to have a mind of their own and the knowledge of whether they are loved (6).

Links with Parents

Listen to parents talking about their very young child. Encourage them to share every detail about their baby's personality, likes and dislikes. Emphasise that this valuable information will help you to tune into their unique child.

Supporting very young children as thinkers during transition

On moving to a childminder or group setting, the appointed key person is primarily responsible for continuing this attachment and attunement, and is not to be a substitute for the parent, but to offer the young child an additional special person.

The age and stage of development of a baby when she moves to a childminder or a group setting may impact on the way she makes a transition. A very young baby may adapt easily to a new carer, but once the baby understands about object and person permanence she is likely to find it more difficult to separate from her parent. The baby now recognises that, although her mum disappears, she is still around somewhere, so why has she abandoned her? Practitioners should be aware that although the baby who comes to them around nine or ten months has enjoyed that extra time with her parent at home, she may take longer to settle happily into a new placement and make a secure secondary attachment.

It is essential that the transition from home is supported. It must help the baby and infant to make a secure attachment to this new special person. The following practices are helpful:

- Encourage the infant to choose his special person. Although a child may initially be 'given' one practitioner to link with, he may warm to someone different. This preferred close relationship is likely to naturally help the baby or infant to settle more easily.
- Provide a transitional object. A very young child experiencing separation needs something that will remind him of the loved parent and home that he has left. A soft, cuddly toy or blanket becomes a comforter and provides the link with the familiar people and things that he is missing in a strange new environment. Personal items from home can be equally comforting, such as mum's scarf which smells of her. Winnicott describes these as 'transitional objects'. They serve a very important role in helping the child to remember home and hold on to his known and secure world while moving into new territory (7).

Questions when working with parents

How clearly and sensitively have I shared with parents the possible challenges for babies and infants when making a transition to my setting?
How well do parents recognise the importance of a 'transitional object' for their very young child?

- Be alert to the needs of the unique child. The quality of the special person relationship has a direct bearing on a very young child's wellbeing and learning. The chemical cortisol, present in all of us, surges in stressful conditions and can close down functions, for example, the child's ability to make connections. When the baby and infant feels loved and cherished, he is relaxed and in the right frame of mind to learn. Penelope Leach offers a cautious warning about the effects of full daycare for children under two years when they are cared for by inexperienced and poorly trained staff. In these circumstances, staff may care dutifully for children's common physical requirements – to be fed, changed and rest – but not be aware of the need for close and intimate interactions which foster the young mind. This approach of treating all children equally can lead to a flatness of effect which is insufficient to support a developing personality (8).

- Ensure that all staff are alerted to each child's needs. Have a display with: a named photograph of each baby and infant, details of his diet, sleep preferences interests and special words he recognises.
- Provide for consistency. A young brain grows through movement, taste, touch, hearing, sight and smell. If these experiences are provided regularly and frequently, connections between brain cells are strengthened. When babies are provided with familiar and consistent routines, this helps them to start to make sense of what is happening to them – they begin to build up a predictable mental structure in their lives. Viewed in this light, the ordinary, daily routines at home and in a group setting, such as feeding, nappy changing and bath time, become significant, but only if they are bespoke to each child. They should be the times when the baby enjoys a warm and responsive relationship with her special person and during these intimate times the key person becomes attuned to the baby's messages. Babies also thrive on these familiar proceedings, gaining confidence in knowing what will happen next. Here is the beginning of sequential thinking.
- Arrange for long-term special relationships. If the special person gets to know her key children intimately, she is tuning in to their thinking. It follows, then, that young children are likely to benefit if they have the same key person over two or three years. This arrangement allows the child to experience the benefits of a long-term, familiar and consistent relationship. The special person is able to follow the child, recognise developmental milestones and understand how his thoughts and ideas are adapted and become more complex over a period of time.

Professional checkpoint

Given the benefits of a young child having a long-term special person who will accompany him as he moves through transitions, how is it possible for this to be organised in a setting?

Professional checkpoint

Recognising the significance of special-person work, what support and guidance do you offer to a new and inexperienced colleague who is about to take on this role in the baby room?

Companionship and communication

In Chapter 1 I suggest that the special person can support the child as a thinking companion. The young child's need for companionship is very well described by Trevarthen:

> Children do need affection and support and protection and so on but they need a lot more than that. They need company which is interested, curious and affectionate. ... Children are very good at private research. They can do it very well, but they don't do it if they are discouraged, if they feel unwanted or lonely then they don't explore. (9)

Offering companionable attention and conversation

Babies and infants are hungry for attention and interest from their special person and will do all they can to communicate. Body language, smiles, gestures and sounds are the baby's initial means of contact. Signing is also a wonderful form of early communication. Very young children will learn to sign their needs and preferences quickly and easily. From six months, babies will learn to sign their choices and needs. Signing is very inclusive. When all young children are encouraged to use sign language, this enables shared communication at a time when many two and three year olds may struggle with words. Signing is sometimes viewed with trepidation by adults – it's yet another skill to master. In fact it is very simple. Signing appears almost effortless for all infants to learn and most move effortlessly on to spoken language. Moreover, when a baby signs she gives us valuable insights into her thoughts.

Communication with babies and infants is dependent on interactions, whether it is a brief smile or a series of exchanges using words and body language, which amount to a conversation. The New Zealand Council for Educational Research published a resource for practitioners which, amidst other helpful guidance, helps them to be aware of the different levels of spoken interaction that occur in settings. These are:

Brief interactions, which include:

- greeting and saying goodbye to the young child
- using language to manage behaviour, such as 'careful' or 'not now'
- comforting a child, such as 'oh dear', 'never mind'
- cursory comments to keep in touch, such as 'well done', 'good boy', 'lovely'

Sustained interactions, which include:

- a focus on something which is interesting to the child
- both adult and child take at least three turns each in a spoken or non-verbal conversation

Very sustained interactions, which are:

- ongoing conversations about a particular idea or way of doing something which can continue over a period of time
- usually linked to a child's schema or topic of interest
- sometimes planned by the adult using a series of connected ideas (10).

Practitioners will use these different types of communication according to the context, the needs of each baby or infant and the practical constraints of time. However, it is the sustained and very sustained interactions that support the child's thinking.

Case Study 3.1

Ben, just 3 years, is digging a hole in the mud.

Ben: 'Look Don, I dug, dug, dug a big hole.'

Don, his key person: 'Just look at that Ben, can you stand in it?'

Ben: [jumping into the hole] 'Oh look, it cover me up.'

Don: 'Not quite Ben, does the hole come up to your tummy?'

Ben: [looking carefully at his tummy and pushing himself up to the side of the hole] 'That's me – I'm big. I'm big, bigger than the hole – it don't cover me, it come up to my tummy.'

Don: 'Yes, I can see that the hole is not big enough to cover you – will you dig some more to make it bigger?'

[Ben shakes his head]

Don: 'What could you do now then?'

Ben: 'I be little.' [crouches down in the hole until he matches the depth of the hole and laughs] 'Now, see the hole cover me up.'

Don: [laughing] 'Oh that's clever – what a good idea.'

Comment

This sustained interaction shows how Don follows Ben's interest and helps him to build on his outside play to gain some insight into relative size. Ben's idea to show that the hole is deep enough to cover him up shows remarkable ingenuity and Don shares his pleasure.

An analysis of research literature from the University of Dundee regarding 'What matters in communicating with babies' identified three influential aspects of parenting/caregiving, namely:

- contingent response where the baby and adult are cueing in to one another and form a mutual understanding

- a rich home literacy environment, which includes shared book reading
- the adult's ability to respond and extend the child's communication (11).

In practical terms, this means the following:

- Personalised contacts with babies and infants mean establishing sensitive and playful channels of communication:
  - o Older babies enjoy playing peek-a-boo and hide and seek games to secure their understandings of object and person permanence.
  - o Most babies around six months relish these games with their special person. They like to play them again and again and in this way they learn that objects hidden can still exist even when you can't see them. They also involve turn-taking, the beginnings of conversations.
  - o Palmer and Bayley (12) offer further some useful points for practitioners and suggest that a literacy focused environment for very young children will include:
    - photographs of themselves, their family members and pets
    - images of familiar toys (a teddy bear) and places (their homes)
    - displayed examples of their mark making with plenty of materials for children to make marks
    - easy access to books.
- Focused and affectionate attention from the adult makes the environment spring to life and impacts on the young child's thinking.

Interactions with infants involve observing their actions, listening to what is spoken and sensitively providing language enrichment to support and extend their thinking. Palmer and Bayley outline some ways to do this.
  Practitioners might:

- Use pole–bridge talk, when you clothe the child's actions in words, modelling some vocabulary but with no pressure on the child to use language. For example:

Child is constructing two towers with blocks:

Adult: Your towers are very tall Sean. Look they are almost as tall as you

- Pick up on the child's comment and expand it. For example:

Child: Mummy gone
Adult: Yes, good bye mummy. Mummy's gone home

- Offer the child a choice of scenarios. For example:

Child: Mummy gone
Adult: Yes, mummy's gone. Is she going shopping or will she call in to see grandma?

The Dundee research group worked with parents to explore some of their issues in communicating with their very young children. They came up with some important messages, some of which are summarised below:

- parents want the best for their children and welcomed suggestions from trusted professionals about communicating with them, but this information is not actively sought out.
- communicating with babies/infants is regarded as simply natural and spontaneous; parents might be encouraged to think about how they weave communication into their companionable and loving relationships.
- parents might overestimate the amount of time they spend talking with their young children.
- information about the rate of early brain development can interest parents and help them to recognise the significance of the first few years of life; they can be helped to see how early communication supports later language development.
- messages for parents need to be succinct and positive, for example *'Your child is so clever already and has a huge capacity to learn'.*

The project findings suggested that discussing these issues with parents can increase awareness of their role as the young child's companion and can change their behaviour (13).

Questions when working with parents

How well do I encourage parents to have easy and natural conversations with their baby using body language as well as talk?
How do I help them practically to carry out this role?

Too often in group settings there are numerous daily routines that can erode the important times for being available and attentive to babies and infants. Elinor Goldschmeid suggested that these times must be a priority and that there should be a protected time or times in the day when a key person gives undivided attention to her very small group of children. She calls this occasion 'the island of intimacy' and suggests that it offers an opportunity for connection and communication in a tranquil atmosphere (14). It should last no longer than 10–12 minutes and, importantly, children should be engaged in something active that interests them (for example, being introduced to a puppet, encouraged to explore a musical box or explore feely boxes, and so on). These types of activity can work well with older two year olds, and it is a cosy and comfortable time when they are introduced to listening and sharing their thoughts with a small group of others. Although some two year olds will be ready to engage briefly with one or two others, this requires a big step in maturation and the key person will recognise if a very young child is not yet ready and is more responsive when given individual attention.

Links with Parents

Model playing simple games with babies and infants when parents are in the setting.
Suggest to parents that they follow up these games at home and let you know how their child responds.
Ask parents to suggest any games that they play with their child at home.
Offer occasional hand-outs with suggestions for games to play at home using everyday household items.

Offering companionable play

An important aspect of special person work is to become the infant's play partner. During the first two years the child's best play resource is the special person whose role is to play with, play alongside or simply to be quietly present observing the bout of play or ready to act as an intermediary to affirm the child's thoughts and ideas.

- Babies thrive on simple 'give and take' games, sharing action rhymes and songs.
- Around two years, infants love close adults to join them in pretend play where they establish the rules and the adult simply follows in a role allotted to them. Very young children will play what they know. If they experience daily routines, such as getting dressed, meal times, sleep times and going to the shops with their carer, they will reflect this in their play. They also observe closely the interests of family members and activities that take place at home and will use these in their play.
- The special person will observe this play and then take part only as and when needed.

Case Study 3.2

Jake, two years, knew that his dad liked fishing although he had never gone fishing with him. Playing with small world figures in the nursery, Jake picked up a teddy saying 'teddy go fishing'. His key person, Rachel, echoed Jake's statement. Jake picked up teddy and took him to the edge of the carpet. 'Is that the water Jake?', asked Rachel. Jake nodded, saying 'water', and then paused for thought. Rachel stayed with the silence and then gently suggests that teddy might need a boat to fish in the water. Jake immediately disappeared and returned with a small car. 'Car boat', he says triumphantly and, placing teddy on top of the car, he pushed it on to the carpet. 'Off he goes into the water', says Rachel, smiling at Jake.

Comment

Rachel supported Jake's play by:

- sitting with him and expressing a quiet interest in his play
- acknowledging his idea about teddy going fishing
- allowing him time to develop his idea
- suggesting a solution when it appears that Jake is finding it difficult to pursue the play
- encouraging Jake's creative response when he transforms the car into a boat.

Offering companionable apprenticeship

Very young children are fascinated by everyday, seemingly mundane household activities, such as making the bed, drying dishes and sorting out cupboards. They are always anxious to help. The special person can encourage an infant to assist, and through chatting about how to go about the task (first we must put all the dirty dishes on this side of the draining board, next I will fill the bowl with hot water and you can put in the washing up liquid) the child will learn sequencing skills. Importantly, she is enjoying being a helper and is relishing in new-found competencies.

Babies and infants also learn a great deal from being with older children. Ideally, they need their own space but also to have opportunities when they can observe and be alongside their older peers. Younger children observe in detail the competencies and skills of older children and this acts as a spur to their own development. They notice and try to copy older children's gross physical skills – running, skipping, jumping – and their fine motor skills – building, mark making and using books. At meal times they see how older children are learning to use cutlery and beakers, and infants will try to perfect these skills alongside them. Integrated age groups also encourage younger children to increase their spoken language as they hear models of talk and try to communicate with more experienced others.

> ## Professional checkpoint
>
> As a special person and companion to an 18 month old, what opportunities do I offer him to develop his thinking competencies as an apprentice?

Climate

As mentioned previously, babies and infants will only strengthen their thoughts and ideas if they have scope to do so. Prime conditions which give this scope include:

- providing for movement, sensory experiences and development of interests
- encouraging scope to re-present
- supporting (but not forcing) independence
- allowing time for the baby and infant to grow, explore, play around with ideas and start to make connections.

Providing for movement, sensory experiences and development of interests

Support meaning-making

Provision for movement and sensing
As babies and infants become more mobile, they need an environment which allows plenty of room for free physical play both inside and outside. Spaces also need to be varied and challenging, encouraging the infant to test moving their bodies in many different ways. Different floor textures and surfaces will challenge the sense of touch. Imaginative and varied outside spaces provide scope for children to climb, roll, spin, and throw. Different ground levels allow them to experience moving their bodies at different speeds and interesting spaces encourage them to view items from different perspectives.

Practical Activity

Provide for mobile babies to encounter different floor textures:

- cover an indoor area with bubble wrap
- plan areas covered with bark chippings, crumpled wrapping paper, shredded newspaper or pieces of fabric
- note the areas when babies choose to linger and return to.

Very young babies use their tongues as a powerful instrument to explore items and then move on to use their hands. At this stage they need easy access to things which they can stroke, cuddle, poke and pick up.

Building on rich sensory experiences, babies and infants become particularly absorbed in patterns of play which are usually linked with movement. Jan White describes the schematic interests that are revealed in two year-old Yasmine's play outside:

> She has some persistent fascinations with moving objects, as well as herself, from one place to another. She seems to be interested in how things can be moved and in movement itself. She prefers to transport resources manually, rather than by filling up buckets and carts. ... Yasmine has linked this passion with an interest in grouping similar things together – perhaps repeatedly grouping and re-grouping her collections enables her to get a better idea of what this means. She uses movement to explore something else she is very curious about, edges and boundaries. ... Yasmine appears to be mapping out the spaces of the nursery garden, getting to know them through her body. (15)

In this example Yasmine is exploring, hypothesising and testing things out. These experiences outside are providing her with the basis of early mathematical and scientific thinking.

Provision for treasure baskets and bags

Once babies can sit up or be propped up with cushions they can be introduced to treasure baskets, a valuable resource which allows for early exploratory play. At this stage, the baby is 'rooted to the spot' and needs stimulus which is within easy reach. The baskets which contain natural items with a variety of textures and shapes are designed to intrigue the baby. Treasure baskets filled with around 12 items provoke the baby to question *'What is this?'* Items from the natural environment provide for more varied exploration rather than manmade or pre-fabricated resources. Elinor Goldschmeid introduced and promoted the use of treasure baskets and has left us with precise guidance on how it should be organised and offered to infants (16).

Treasure bags offer an infant a different dimension – the element of surprise. Now the items are not visible and the infant plunges her hand into the bag, feels different textures, sizes and shapes and selects something to pull out and explore. At first the choice is quite random, but if the same bag of items is offered again and again, the infant uses her sense of touch to remind her of what is there and she will start to deliberately search for a preferred item.

Provision for heuristic play

Mobile infants will enjoy heuristic play. The term 'heuristic' comes from the Greek word 'eurisko', which means 'to discover or gain an understanding of' (17). In simple terms, heuristic play is when they investigate collections of small items and transfer them into larger containers. Here the infant's question moves to *'What is this for?'* In order to find out, the infant tests out the properties of the items through sorting, selecting, filling and dropping them. They discover that items can be used in different ways – wooden pegs can be attached to a piece of cardboard but wooden sticks cannot. Some items behave in similar ways – cotton reels and small soft balls can roll. Infants will repeat their investigations again and again until they have satisfied their discoveries and so start to make connections.

In heuristic play, space should be sufficient for infants to move around and make their discoveries without coming into contact with other children. Blocks of time should allow for babies and infants to pursue their investigations without interruption. The adult is always nearby, but this time as an observer rather than a play partner. She will note what particularly intrigues the infant and when they have had enough and lose interest, using these observations to plan future provision.

When parents are encouraged to bring items from home which are of interest to the baby, these can be added to a treasure basket or heuristic play. These 'known items' provide the very young child with precious and reassuring links with their family.

Provision for schema
A young child may commonly show his thoughts and interests through repeated patterns of behaviour or schema.

- **Become aware**: if parents and practitioners become familiar with categories of schema (see Chapter 2), it helps them to recognise how a child's behaviour fits into a particular scheme. It also helps close adults to make sense of an activity which otherwise might appear as a series of disconnected events.
- **Provide**: once the special person has observed these patterns of schematic behaviour, she can deepen and enrich the infant's focused interest through providing additional stimulus either through adding resources or adapting space. For example, infants who transport need access to bags, buckets, trolleys and wheelbarrows to move smaller items around. Those with an interest in enveloping need materials to wrap up items, hidey holes, dens, large boxes and improvised tents to hide away objects or themselves. Infant transporters and envelopers need clear spaces in which to strengthen these interests.
- **Adapt**: as schema spotting becomes a focus for observation, the child's special person begins to recognise how she might help to link one scheme with another or change her focus as the infant follows a new interest. She becomes familiar with the child's new emerging thoughts and ideas.

Case Study 3.3

Lisa, 18 months, was preoccupied pushing a wooden trolley up and down the corridor at home. She was also very attached to a soft toy dog on wheels which she took for a walk. Her mum observed these transporting schema, picked up the toy dog and placed it in the trolley saying 'doggie wants a ride in your trolley'.

The next day Lisa started her journey pushing the trolley and then stopped. She searched around, found the dog and placed it carefully in the trolley. Lisa turned to her mum and gave her a big grin.

Comment

Lisa's mum had helped Lisa to connect two aspects of her interests in transporting. Lisa readily included the dog in her trolley (she could equally have thrown the dog out! It's important to recognise when the child interprets support as interference and rejects a suggestion). The next day Lisa recalled this new idea and included the dog in her play.

The development of spoken language around 18 months gives further clues into the young child's interests. The special person will note words that are frequently repeated and items that are labelled.

Professional checkpoint

How far do I plan content for treasure baskets, bags and heuristic play to link with early schematic interests?

Professional checkpoint

Sue works in a setting which caters for a mixed age group (2–4 year olds) within one large room. She sets up a role-play area which is well used by the older children, but a group of two year old transporters repeatedly move resources out of the role-play area and reduce the environment to chaos.

How can Sue best support the schematic concerns of the two year olds while protecting the needs of older children for sustained imaginative play?

Links with Parents

Familiarise parents with schema through:

- displaying examples of common schema demonstrated in children's play
- providing a simple booklet which describes common schema
- explaining that schemes of thinking can also apply to adults and be reflected in aspects of their lives, for example, the ways in which they organise items in cupboards, store their clothes, their workspace preferences.

Encourage parents to spot their very young child's dominant schema at home as this will help them to understand some reasons behind some patterns of behaviour.
Provide them with further activities and stories which can feed their child's schema.

Provision for interests gained through screen media
Introducing very young children to computers, TV and DVD is seen by many as a dubious practice and the American Academy of Paediatrics suggested that babies under one year should not be exposed to viewing (18). Even though resources have been developed and refined since then, this recommendation seems to be sensible. However, the reality of modern life means that many children are exposed to the screen very early in life, either with the television switched on in the background or to view certain programmes. On average, two and three year olds in America have one or two hours' viewing experience daily. If we know that very young children are viewing digital programmes, practitioners should be well informed about possible gains and damaging consequences from the experience and be able to offer guidance to parents.

Studies show that by 12 months, infants can and do learn from watching good-quality TV and DVD programmes (19) but only when certain conditions are met. Positive viewing is helped when:

- there is lots of repetition which enables infants to predict what will happen next
- the content is familiar and infants can view everyday events which they recognise in their lives
- there is an element of humour and fun which adds to enjoyment
- objects shown move dynamically across the whole screen, enabling the infant's need to move their eyes in order to follow movements
- high contrast colours clearly separate foreground from background

- the viewing time is brief (5–10 minutes) and the programme is stopped once the child is no longer interested
- the programme invites participation through movement, sounds and words.

Meeting the above criteria will ensure that programmes are more likely to help the infant's attention and help him to gain information from the screen, but the most important addition is the child's special person, who acts as a co-viewer. In this role, the adult will share the child's interest and enjoyment in the programme, listening and following his reactions and comments. She will point and describe items and help him link the content to his own known experiences (20).

Figure 3.1

This image of big and little batman reflects two year-old Flora's interest in super-hero characters she had encountered in picture books and in DVDs she had viewed with her mum, dad and sister.

Encouraging scope to represent

Infants will happily represent their world with anything that is available to them. Ordinary household objects will be used to meet their purposes.

The infant needs space to move around safely and use what she needs to convey her thoughts and ideas. She will use materials at hand to imitate actions observed – a shoe becomes a mobile phone and a tea towel a shawl. At this stage, representing can be messy – infants will move fluidly in their play, using and dropping items and sometimes leaving a trail of debris. This is not a time to insist on clearing up. Practitioners will recognise that serious learning is happening as infants select, investigate and discard things as they seek what they need to make sense. The adult's role again is to observe and occasionally to add high-quality resources which offer scope for fantasy play:

- With adult encouragement infants will play peek-a-boo games, hiding small world figures and favourite soft toys.
- Babies and infants love books and early, happy experiences of stories will enrich early pretend play. If small-scale figures are available, they will be incorporated into pretend stories, as will any available items. Very young children do not build dens but they will seek out private spaces in which to hide and imagine. Spaces behind sofas and under tables are favourite hidey holes where an infant can become engrossed in her private world of make-believe.
- Cardboard boxes offer tremendous scope for imaginative ventures. Without any prompting, mobile babies and infants will use large boxes as hidey holes and enjoy moving in and out of them or taking treasured possessions in with them.
- Given thick pens and paints, they will mark-make and cover surfaces with colour. After initial exploration and with increased confidence using boxes, older infants may transform them to reflect aspects of their experience – a bus, a car, a boat. If practitioners know about children's interests, they can support the play, taking care to follow the young child's lead. However, many infants will not be ready for this more elaborate play until they have had more time to become familiar with the possibilities that boxes hold.

Links with Parents

How do I help parents recognise:

- the need to limit exposure to screen-based media?
- ways to support their very young child's viewing of TV/DVD?
- the importance of simple, open-ended materials for early exploration?

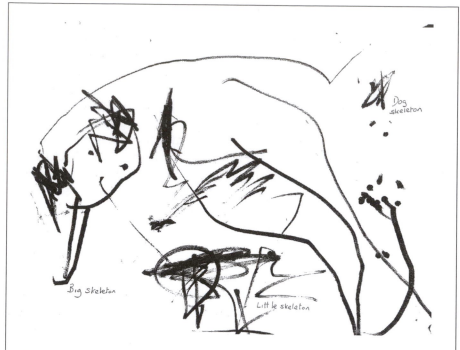

Figure 3.2

Around the time of Halloween Flora had become very interested in skeletons displayed in shop windows. Her mum read her the story of *Funny Bones*, a great favourite. Later Flora produced this image when drawing alongside her older sister. She pointed to and named each of the characters in turn.

Encouraging early intentions

Given the opportunity, babies and infants start to show clear intentions about what they wish to see, consider and do. This persistent and determined behaviour signals the very young child as a 'going concern', growing and developing every minute, as she builds up her model of a world that she can understand (21). Close adults have the fascinating task of observing and building on each child's unfolding understanding. They work as social constructivists, acting as thinking companions. They support and encourage the very young child's early intentions, encouraging the child's moves to become self-sufficient in controlling or regulating her thinking and feelings. Bronson suggests that three components of self-regulation are: to organise information so that it makes sense; to predict events; and to find a more fascinating way to solve a problem (22).

Close adults can observe and encourage these moves by:

- noting where very young children link their schema and encouraging them to make connections in their thinking
- recognising and affirming when infants start to recognise simple patterns and anticipate what is going to happen next during the daily routine, for example, recognise signs of preparation for snack time
- giving children scope to come up with their own solutions, for example, the practitioner stood back when Roxanne couldn't find her hat to wear outside. Roxanne solved the problem by emptying the waste paper basket and placing it on her head.

Children will stand a good chance of becoming self-regulated in an environment which encourages them to think and act for themselves and to have time to consider their thoughts and actions.

Supporting independence

When babies and infants are in a predictable and known environment they become familiar with the layout of the surroundings, the resources available to them and the organisation of the day. This gives them confidence and a sense of control over what they are doing which is fundamental to help them branch out. However, it's a matter of balance – an unchanging environment and inflexible, humdrum routines with no surprises result in a bored child and a ceiling being placed on their thinking. Very young babies are necessarily dependent on their caregivers for their physical needs. Nevertheless, an important aspect of young children being 'going concerns' involves them making choices and decisions which means them learning to think carefully about options. Provision should present choices which enable this to happen:

- A one year old needs scope to select what he wants to eat, where he wants to move around, and when he needs to sleep. The accessible range of resources around, provided through treasure baskets and bags and heuristic play and through continuous provision, will allow him to see what is available and decide what he wants to explore and investigate.
- A year later, there is surge of independence. By the time the child is two she starts to understand that she can cause things to happen and is beginning to assert her independence in thought and action. She will start to make her own decisions, show preferences and sometimes refuse to comply. This new-found move to autonomy means that the special person, while continuing to provide the firm anchor of security, will balance this with times when she stands back to allow space for the child to move forward.

- Two year olds sometimes assert their newly found autonomy by becoming defiant and refusing to co-operate. The special person will aim to avoid these collisions by providing an infrastructure which allows children to do things for themselves and achieve physical competence. Instead of the adult wiping children's mouths after lunch, provision of a mirror on a stand and a box of tissues will encourage infants to cope with this small routine themselves and give them a sense of control.

- At this age the sequence of getting dressed can be a serious problem-solving activity. The special person will maintain an unobtrusive presence to ensure that the child has just sufficient help if he cannot cope. She will have encouraged the child to undress and leave his clothes in an orderly pile. When dressing, this helps him to apply his sequential thinking and replace each item of clothing in the right order, achieving a heady feeling of competency. The skilful adult ensures that it is possible for the child to achieve mastery:

  - at first, with the adult providing physical assistance and talking through the routine
  - next, with some help and encouraging the child to talk through the routine
  - increasing the amount that the child does for himself and encouraging signs of self-dressing skills
  - ensuring that the child is able to practise and apply new self-dressing skills in his own time.

Professional checkpoint

How well do I balance a predictable programme with new experiences to interest and intrigue very young children?

Allowing time

The powerful evidence from neuroscience that babies think and that adults can aid this process may lead to questionable practices of hot-housing very young children. Eager parents, wishing to push their infants on to the ladder of success, can easily find a market of materials which promise impressive results. Nutbrown and Page warn against this trend and quote an example of one survey from the USA which shows that 65% of parents believe that flashcards are very effective in helping two year olds develop their intellectual capacity (23). A wise comment from Sue Gerhardt counters this enthusiasm, as she argues for the prime importance of social contact:

> The first higher brain capacities to develop are social, and they develop in response to social experience. Rather than holding up flashcards to a baby, it would be more appropriate to the baby's stage of development to simply hold him and enjoy him (24).

Time is a precious commodity and in this hurry-along world it constantly seems to be in short supply. Practitioners are only too aware that there is a great deal to be done during the working day and sometimes, in an attempt to 'fit' everything in, the daily programme is fragmented into segments – greeting time, play time, nappy change, snack, play outside, rest, and so on. This programmed approach can create stress for adults, who can fall into the trap of clock-watching to make sure that they keep to time. Most importantly, although a fragmented and inflexible programme may provide a structure for practitioners, it does not meet the needs of babies and infants. Gopnik makes the message clear: 'An animal that depends on imagination has to have some time to exercise it. Childhood is that time'. (25)

Babies and infants offer many non-verbal messages which signal their needs, if only we are prepared to listen to them. Petrie and Owen consider valuable messages from a renowned early years specialist Magda Gerba who argued strongly that adults should observe and listen closely to young children and take a lead from them. The baby is regarded as active and competent to take initiatives (26). In practice Gerba suggests that this means allowing a baby to develop motor skills unencumbered by props. For example, instead of providing a baby chair at meal times, a baby who cannot sit at the table independently is fed on the lap of the key person and responds to a close one-to-one relationship. Moreover, the adult does not determine a set meal time. The baby is only fed when he signals that he is hungry. At other times babies and infants are encouraged to develop and practise emerging motor skills in their own time. The adult does not intervene but stays near and notes the baby's preferences to move around and reach out for objects. Gerba argues strongly for babies and infants to grow and develop when they are ready. She reasons that infants always do what they can do – and they should not be expected to do what they are not ready for. Moreover, that every infant develops according to his or her built in predetermined time schedule (27). Crain echoes this message to follow the child's time:

> Children enter the world with an inborn growth schedule that is the product of several million years of biological evolution. They are pre-eminently 'wise' about what they need and what they are ready and not ready to do.

... If baby is hungry, we should feed her; if she wants to play, we should go ahead and play with her; if she is sleepy we should let her sleep and not rouse her to be fed. The baby follows nature's laws so we can safely follow the baby's cues. (28)

Going along with this principle of listening to the child, the special person will carefully observe the child's schematic interests and plan to extend these. In order to develop and give birth to their thoughts and try out their ideas, very young children need chunks of unhurried time. This time allows their experiences to fall into place, link with what they have found out already and become meaningful. There is not always a neat, finished product, but the thinking processes are alive and powerful.

Case Study 3.4

Nichola, 26 months, had recently joined the nursery and had Polish as a first language. He settled into the setting and persistently chose to ride a tricycle in a circle outdoors. His special person, Rick, observed this repetitive activity on five consecutive days. On the sixth morning, Rick assembled a large container of open unit blocks inside and started building a circle with the curved ones. On entering the nursery that morning Nichola noticed this activity and paused to watch. Rick simply said hello and continued to build. Nichola edged forward and sat down. 'Would you like to help me Nichola?' asked Rick, and placed a curved block into his hand. Nichola threw away the block but remained sitting. Rick moved away to greet another child and when he returned Nichola was absorbed in continuing to construct the circle. Rick brought over a box of small vehicles which he placed nearby. Nichola ignored this resource, but continued building that day and for the rest of the week. He later happily used large plastic hoops to add to his construction.

Comment

Rick based his support for Nichola on observation over a period of time and deduced that Nichola was interested in a rotational scheme. Rick introduced the open unit blocks in order to extend Nicholas's horizon for play indoors and to provide more content for his interest. He encouraged Nichola to accommodate the block building in his own way and in his own time.

It's very rare for new thoughts and ideas to come to us instantaneously. Despite knowing this, we can be impatient, expecting a rapid response from a baby or infant to experiences he has been offered. We fail to understand that new ideas need time to be accommodated and then assimilated.

Case Study 3.5

Ruth's mum took her three year old daughter to see a performance of *The Snowman* at a London theatre. Ruth was familiar with the story but this was her first experience of seeing a live performance. The little girl appeared absorbed during the show but said very little afterwards. Her mother admitted to being disappointed at the lack of response but did not press Ruth for a reaction.

About two weeks later it snowed heavily and unexpectedly in the night. When Ruth woke up and looked out of the window she rushed to get dressed and, refusing to have any breakfast, she insisted in going outside. Ruth set to making a snowman and took great care to represent every detail of the character she had seen on stage. She asked her mum for a carrot for his nose, buttons for his eyes, a scarf and hat. Ruth worked tirelessly to represent her snowman and reluctantly agreed to go inside after two hours of solid work. She then talked excitedly about the adventures that she would share with the snowman and how the next day she would build the snowman's friend. Her mum listened carefully throughout as Ruth re-told the story.

The temperature rose during the night and Ruth discovered that the snowman had disappeared. She turned to mum cheerfully saying 'I thought that might happen – my snowman has flown to join his friend in the sky and they will have such fun together'.

Comment

Ruth's experience of seeing *The Snowman* lay dormant until the snow outside triggered a connection with the story. When building the snowman, Ruth recalled and imitated what she had seen. But more than that, by introducing the snowman's friend and providing a happy resolution, Ruth instigated her own thoughts and ideas. Her mum had enabled this to happen by allowing time for these thought processes to grow and providing companionship and resources when the moment was right.

Professional checkpoint

How far do the organisational demands of our daily programme interrupt the young child's need to pursue interests in their own time?

> ## Key points for working with parents
>
> Help parents to understand:
>
> - the importance of observing their baby and infant closely in order to recognise what interests and absorbs them
> - the value of simple household items which can be used in early symbolic play.
>
> Share examples of how the very young child makes connections in her thinking and conveys this at home and in the setting.
>
> Suggest to parents that they:
>
> - encourage their baby and infant to become involved with them in daily chores and gradually allow them to do more as they become proficient
> - try to allow unhurried time for the child to achieve as much as possible for herself.

Useful stories

Bratney, S. and Jeram, A. (2007) *Guess How Much I Love You*. London: Walker Books.
A story about unconditional love.

Lamb, A. and McPhail, D. (2011) *Tell Me the Day Backwards*. Massachusetts: Candlewick Press.
A delightful story which helps infants recall events in their day and encourages sequential thinking.

Melling, D. (2004) *Just Like My Mum*. London: Hodder & Stoughton.
Melling, D. (2007) *Just Like My Dad*. London: Hodder & Stoughton.
A little lion cub wants to do things like his mum and dad. A lovely example of companionable apprenticeship.

References

1. Robinson, M. (2003) *From Birth to One: The Year of Opportunity*. Oxford: Oxford University Press, p. 128.
2. Read, V. (2010) *Developing Attachment in Early Years Settings*. London: Routledge, p. 17.
3. Robinson (2003) *From Birth to One* (see note 1), p. 11.
4. Siraj-Blatchford, I. (2011) 'How Adults Can Support Young Children's Learning at Home and at Pre-school'. Presentation at Hants Early Years Conference, February.
5. Roberts, R. (2010) *Well-Being from Birth*. London: Sage, pp. 58–64.
6. Robinson (2009) 'Communicating and Babbling' in *The Year of Wonder* (2009), Newcastle: Siren Films, p.11.

7. Winnicott, D.W. (1965) *The Maturation Process and the Facilitating Environment.* London: Karnac.
8. Leach, P., Stein, A. and Sylva, K. (2005) *Families, Children and Childcare Study.* London: Institute of Children, Families and Social Issues, Birkbeck College, University of London.
9. Trevarthen, C. (1988), quoted in P. Elfer, E. Goldschmeid and D. Selleck (2003) *Key Persons in the Nursery.* London: David Fulton, p.11.
10. Dunkin, D. and Hannan, P. (2001) *Thinking Together.* Wellington: New Zealand Council for Educational Research, p. 3.
11. Hamer, C. (2011) 'Face to Face', *Early Education*, 63 (Spring): pp.10–11.
12. Palmer, S. and Bayley, R. (2004) *Foundations of Literacy.* Stafford: Network Educational Press.
13. Hamer (2011) 'Face to Face' (see note 11).
14. Jackson, S. (2009) 'Close to You', *Nursery World*, 30 April, pp. 22/23.
15. White, J. (2010) *Toddlers Outdoors, Play Learning and Development.* Newcastle: Siren Films Ltd, pp. 24–5.
16. Goldschmeid, E. (1987) *Infants at Work.* Video. London: National Children's Bureau.
17. Goldschmeid, E. and Hughes, A. (1992) *Heuristic Play with Objects: Children of 12–20 Months Exploring Everyday Objects.* Video. London: National Children's Bureau.
18. Entin, E. (2011) 'Toddlers and TV: The American Academy of Paediatrics says No', available at: www.theatlantic.com/health/archive/2011/10 (accessed 31 October 2011).
19. Karmiloff, K. and Karmiloff-Smith, A. (2010) 'TV Times', *Nursery World*, 17 February, pp. 22–3.
20. Courage, M.L. and Setliff, A.E. (2010) 'When Babies Watch Television: Attention-getting, Attention-holding, and the Implications for Learning from Video Material', *Developmental Review*, 30: 220–38.
21. Winnicott, D.W. (1964) *The Child, the Family and the Outside World.* Harmondsworth: Penguin.
22. Bronson, M. (2000) *Self-Regulation in Early Childhood: Nature and Nurture.* New York: Guilford Press, p. 149.
23. Nutbrown, C. and Page, J. (2008) *Working with Babies and Children from Birth to Three.* London: Sage, p. 10.
24. Gerhardt, S. (2004) *Why Love Matters.* London: Sage, p. 38.
25. Gopnik, A. (2009) *The Philosophical Baby.* London: Bodley Head, p. 10.
26. Petrie, S. and Owen, S. (2005) *Authentic Relationships in Group Care for Infants and Toddlers: Resources for Infant Educators (RIE) Principles into Practice.* London: Jessica Kingsley.
27. Evans, M. (2010) 'Learning and Development: Taking Inspiration from Magda Gerba', *Nursery World*, 25 August, pp. 16–17.
28. Crain, W. (2003) *Reclaiming Childhood: Letting Children Be Children in Our Achievement-Oriented Society.* New York: Henry Holt, pp. 11–12.

Playing with Thoughts and Ideas: Young Children's Thinking 3–5 Years

---

Intentions

This chapter:

- recognises how children's dispositions to think are influenced by their sense of self and in relationships with others
- acknowledges our understanding of how children:
  - continue to make sense of experiences through their schema, in play, connecting their ideas and through early representations
  - develop and use language to share thoughts and ideas with adults and peers
  - learn further to self-regulate their behaviour and become intentional thinkers

---

Given a loving and supportive introduction into the world, by three years of age most children are active and experienced thinkers. In this chapter we consider how children strengthen their dispositions and aptitudes to think, and develop and extend their thinking further through their growing powers of communication, investigation, reason and imagination.

These aspects of development in thinking are all part of young children learning to self-regulate. Self-regulation is described as 'a deep internal mechanism that enables children as well as adults to engage in mindful, intentional and thoughtful behaviours' (1). We saw in the previous chapter that this process starts very early. The Tickell Review recognises that self-regulation is a significant influence on becoming an effective lifelong learner (2). Bodrova and Leong support this and suggest that emotional self-regulation and cognitive self-regulation appear to have come from the same roots. This means that as children mature they can increasingly be in control of their thinking and their feelings. And the more that they take control, the better they become at doing so. On the other hand, if young children do not learn how to self-regulate, their potential for mindful, thoughtful and intentional behaviours is likely to be stunted (3).

Developing a disposition to think

Attachments and early mind-sets

The primacy of a sound attachment during the earliest years of life has already been stressed – babies and infants need to feel understood, loved and cared for in order to start to move out and explore the world around them. The firing of connections between brain cells and subsequent filaments of thought are dependent on this early, bespoke care.

Older children continue to need sound attachments, where these close relationships help the child to build a view of herself and then to place a value on her identity. The way in which she sees herself and develops her self-esteem is linked to the relationships that she has with close family members and her key person. Four year-old Alison's self-esteem is mainly secure as she recognises that she is valued in different ways by her daddy, her baby brother and in the nursery. She has a lower self-esteem though when she is with her older brother, who makes it clear that she is often a nuisance and interferes with his play. Alison is beginning to see where she fits in or belongs in her family group.

We recognise that a child with a sound self-esteem is well placed to think and learn. Positive self-esteem, though, is not sufficient in itself – self-knowledge is also important. The child not only has an optimistic view of herself, but starts to recognise what she is good at and what is a struggle. However, in order to think and learn, young children must believe that they are able to do so. If this belief is not secured during the early years of life, it's more difficult for it to blossom later.

Case Study 4.1

I was visiting a reception class when Rose, playing with small world resources, asked me the purpose of my visit. I explained that I wanted to look at children's drawings and paintings.

(Continued)

(Continued)

Rose nodded understandingly and said: 'Oh, mine aren't very good – you need to look at Keiran's pictures – he's really, really clever at drawing.' Then she paused and smiled. 'But I'm ace at changing for PE and my teacher says so.'

Comment

Rose had high self-esteem and, with affirmation from her teacher, recognised what she did well. Because she was secure, she was able to generously acknowledge those who had greater talents than her.

The initial drive to find out, explore and investigate that is so evident in babies is tempered by three or four years of experience. We now recognise those young children who are positively motivated to think and learn, who persevere and persist with queries, and those others who are more hesitant and distractible.

As we have seen with babies, feelings can have a profound effect on thinking and learning and this continues in life. Siegler et al. suggest that 'how children think and feel about themselves plays a role in how they respond to their successes and failures' (4). Dweck supports this view and illustrates it by her reference to mastery and helpless behaviour (5). Children who follow a mastery approach are confident and have a positive view of themselves. They relish new, challenging experiences and believe that they can succeed even in the face of difficulty. Other children are unsure of themselves. Because they lack self-belief, they constantly look for approval from others. These children show helpless behaviour; they give up easily and when things go wrong they believe that it is their own fault because 'they are no good'. Dweck suggests that the master learners develop a growth mind-set; they wrestle with problems and delight in the effort of thinking and learning. Much of their pleasure lies in the process of thinking, grappling with, assimilating and accommodating ideas. Duckworth and colleagues summarise how master learners persist in their enquiries and show 'grit' in their determination to succeed (6).

The helpless learners adopt a fixed mind-set; they stick to the familiar where they can feel safe and they know what to do – they are reluctant to try anything new. Those with a fixed mind-set avoid the challenge of uncertainty and initial confusion involved with thinking (7). Although Dweck's work refers to older children and adults, these early patterns of behaviour emerge with three and four year olds as they begin to recognise who they are and what they can do. The consequences of negative self-esteem in the early years can be profound as children move into school and reject facing the effort involved in thinking and learning. Their helpless mind-set means that they are unable to adopt strategies to help themselves.

Dweck's descriptors of mastery and helpless patterns of behaviour and positive and growth mind-sets are closely linked to young children's dispositions to think and how these dispositions are reflected in behaviour.

Carr and Claxton acknowledge that there are a number of dispositions which support thinking and learning but select three most important ones for practitioners to observe. These are summarised below:

- **Resilience**: the tendency to persist despite setbacks and frustrations and take on thinking challenges where the outcome is uncertain.
- **Playfulness**: the willingness to adapt situations, to mull over ideas and be creative in interpreting and responding to problems.
- **Reciprocity**: to share ideas and thoughts with other adults and children in a social relationship. (8, 9)

These dispositions resonate closely with Freire Laevers' scales for involvement and well-being. For Laevers, involvement is shown by the child's concentrated perseverance, a strong flow of energy and a drive to explore. He describes the outcomes of well-being as enjoyment, relaxation, vitality, openness, self-confidence and being in touch with oneself (10). When young children achieve high scores on involvement and well-being, their resilience and playfulness are apparent and this is evident in many social scenarios.

Case Study 4.2

Elise attended a church school and the local vicar took a service in the school once a week.

Elise's reception teacher, Sarah, was keen to help children become aware of themselves as thinkers. She encouraged them to use their 'thinking brains' to try to solve problems or questions that puzzled them.

Elise approached Sarah one day saying that she had a question. 'There is God the Father, God the Son and God the Holy Ghost – how can that be?' Sarah, somewhat taken aback by this sudden question, said that she would like time to think further about it.

'No', said Elise firmly, 'you see I've been thinking very hard. I have a daddy and I'm his little daughter. I have a little brother and I'm his big sister and I have a grandma and I'm her grandson' (she corrected herself quickly) 'no, I'm her granddaughter. So you see, it all fits together.'

(Continued)

(Continued)

Comment

In grappling with this very difficult question Elise had absorbed (assimilated) the notion of one deity being interpreted in three ways. She puzzled over how this could be possible and drew a parallel or connection with her own family circumstances. By doing this, Elise adjusted (accommodated) this new notion to her understanding.

Two weeks previously Elise had shared her question with her mother. However, she refused to discuss it, saying that she needed to think hard about it by herself. Her mum reported that, during the intervening weeks, Elise had seemed quiet and preoccupied and was heard talking to her teddy a lot.

The process of mental disequilibrium clearly took some time, but Elise showed a positive mind-set and seemed to relish the challenge of thinking. She was resilient in persisting with the problem, playful in mulling over her ideas and coming up with a creative response. Once she had resolved her question she was keen to share it with Sarah.

Social understandings: thinking with other children

In Chapter 2 we saw how babies and infants become very socially aware within contacts with close family members. As young children develop, their social horizons and their friendships become increasingly important. And, once again, play is a critical context.

> Children are engaged in mutual exchanges and learn how to interact with each other and others. (11)

By three and four years, children are really keen to play with other children. Dunn suggests that in these new social relationships children learn a great deal about others and think about how to be with them. This includes learning how to conciliate, negotiate and give and take in order to maintain the play. They are also more likely to share their thoughts and feelings with their friends (12).

Thinking can be a solitary activity but our ideas and thoughts expand when we are with others. Vygotsky strongly supported social learning; he claimed that mental activity begins with social contacts and exchanges between people, including young children. Eventually, the child takes on these exchanges and will use conversation as a basis for her own thinking. Vygotsky suggested that what the child does in co-operation with others, she eventually learns to do alone (13). Young children can learn a great deal from being with adults, but so often a relationship of authority and dependence can erode a child's confidence. When relating to other children the contacts are equal. By four and five years, children select their own groups and they choose to work with others who share their interests or schemes of thinking. Cath Arnold found that children made these choices in her family group at the Penn Green Centre. She also noticed that when disputes arose, this was often because their interest or schemas conflicted (14). My own observations of four year old boys revealed some enduring friendships and shared thinking from pairs of boys who shared the same schema.

Making sense

Consolidating and extending schemes of thinking

By three years of age children will have had many experiences and developed their preoccupations or 'schemes of thinking' by repeating actions again and again. If babies and infants have been encouraged to investigate things of interest and patterns of movement, these repeated encounters can lead to early understandings of basic concepts. In Chapter 2 we mentioned some common types of schema. Table 4.1 outlines some common schema and how they start to link into concepts in areas of learning in the Early Years Foundation Stage (EYFS).

Table 4.1   Links between some common schema and concepts in areas of learning in the Early Years Foundation Stage

Early schemes of thinking	Understanding of basic concepts in the EYFS
Rotating	Objects and actions that turn (**Understanding the world: Technology**)
Enveloping	Creating/occupying a space, covering and containing objects or themselves in a space (**Mathematics: Shape, space and measures**)
Enclosing	Use ideas, involving fitting, overlapping, in, out enclosure, grids and sun like shapes (**Expressive arts and design: Exploring and using media and materials**)
Positioning	Placement/lining up of objects (**Mathematics: Shape, space and measures/numbers**)
Trajectory	How things and people move and how movements can be changed (**Physical: Moving and handling**)

As young children develop several interests, they begin to combine and connect their schema and make connections in their thinking. For example, Alex, at three years, was absorbed in covering and enveloping himself in different materials; he subsequently became interested in enclosing himself in small spaces and in small world play he enclosed groups of animals in pens using blocks and planks. He started to line up the animals in two or three symmetrical rows and told his special person that 'these must look the same'. Alex's enveloping schema had led to him developing other closely related interests which formed a schema cluster. For over two months this particular cluster dominated Alex's play.

Importantly, young children's schema develop through allowing them access to their favourite types of play. This is when they are most likely to be highly motivated, involved and disposed to think.

Social scripts

One way in which children learn to place their world into an intelligible framework is by using 'generalised event representations' or social scripts to describe everyday events (15). Children experience daily routines at home, such as getting dressed, eating and going to the shops. In the nursery, their programme is predictable with times for play, snack, washing hands, stories and songs. As they become familiar with these routines they built a 'script' of events. The detail included in each of the events will vary according to the child's experience and stage of development. Infants already memorise events as they recall and construct an early mental script. For instance, two year old Anna remembered where to find the bag of flour in the cupboard when she was making cakes with her mum. Older children's scripts become more elaborate and may be embellished by stories they have heard and TV programmes and DVDs they have seen. Typically, they involve a sequence of scenes which help them to recall activities, places and relationships and place them in a frame of reference. Scripts help the child to feel in control of what he or she experiences and to predict the pattern of the day rather than passively wait for things to happen. Other significant findings relating to scripts indicate that where children are particularly interested in events they tend to represent them in greater detail, and as they become very familiar with an event the represented script becomes more consistent and secure. A longitudinal study of young French children's scripts of their nursery school events showed a clear progression. Three year old children's scripts were not clearly established, but the scripts of four and five year olds were better organised, sequenced and more elaborate (16).

Case Study 4.3

I visited a reception class three days after children had started school. I wanted to find out how much of an understanding children had about school in this short space of time. I approached Gavin and asked him: 'What do you do in this school?' He paused for thought and then told me: 'Well, we paint and draw and go outside to play. Sometimes we have a story and we must try to sit and cross our legs'. After another pause, Gavin continued: 'That's not all. We have lunch and then we go to the hall. I like that. We have to take off our clothes and put them together, 'cos they will get lost. Then our mummies come to take us home.' Over the other side of the class I approached Joe with the same question. Joe avoided looking at me. He simply hung his head and muttered: 'I dunno, I dunno.'

Comment

After only three days in school Gavin has already got a wonderfully clear grasp of some main school events. His detailed and well-sequenced script and understanding of what is required shows that he is rapidly feeling himself to be a member of the class community. Joe, on the other hand, is lost. He is unable to describe to me aspects of his life in school because at this stage he has no clear understanding. Things happen during the course of the day over which he feels he has no control. For Joe, school life is still a buzzing and unpredictable confusion; he needs considerable support from a caring adult to help him devise a mental framework of his school experiences.

Dowling, M. (2009) *Young Children's Personal, Social and Emotional Development*. London: Sage, p. 56.

Pretend and fantasy play

We have seen in Chapter 2 how older infants start to use symbols to represent things in their play and create pretend stories. This move towards abstract thought strengthens as children become more experienced players. Children's social scripts involve real events whereas when young children make stories they move into make-believe. However, both scripts and stories help children to organise information in their brains. Fernyhough suggests that:

> where story really makes a difference is in the way it gives toddlers a handle on time. For a child trying to understand herself as an entity with a past, a present and a future, keeping track of what happened, and when must be a formidable challenge. Story gives her a structure in which she can order these ideas in sequence. (17)

Having said that, young three year olds are not always concerned with recounting a strict order of events, but may weave a story which has a very loose time framework:

> By anticipating the future course of action in their make believe, children exchange and develop a wealth of thoughts about different situations, none of which are witnessed but which are imaginable. (18)

Case Study 4.4

While three year old Emily was with her childminder she had watched a video of Mickey Mouse with immense enjoyment. She was also aware that when she was with the childminder her mother had been having driving lessons and had very recently passed her driving test. Emily lived by the coast where, during the summer months, she often watched a Punch and Judy show with her mother. Emily shared this script with me.

> When I'm big I'm going to have a Mickey Mouse car and Mickey Mouse sunglasses and Mickey Mouse lipstick. You can come in my car and sit in the front but you must do up your seat belt. But first I must have driving lessons, lots and lots – to pass my test. We shall go ... go to Punch and Judy. I like Mr Punch, but not the devil, he frightens me.

Comment

Emily skilfully drew on all of these experiences as she portrayed a future script for herself. She draws on knowledge she has acquired about learning to drive and being safe in a car, the trappings needed to assume the role of Mickey Mouse and she revisits both the pleasures and fears of the Punch and Judy show. This is a mature script which Emily has developed into an imaginative story where she envisages her future.

Vivian Paley's rich first-hand accounts of children's fantasy play provide secure evidence of the power of this natural means of learning. Paley asserts that:

> There is no activity for which young children are better prepared than fantasy play. Nothing is more dependable and risk-free and the dangers are only pretend. ... It is in the development of their themes and characters and plots that children explain their thinking and enable us to wonder who we might become as their teachers. (19)

In their play children take on different roles and explore and discuss possibilities. They also appropriate language and try it out for size. Four year old Jake, playing with two other boys as estate agents, announced firmly and with authority that 'our shop is a multinational company'. It was soon apparent that he did not really understand what the term meant, but he had heard it used at home and recognised that it meant big and important.

Case Study 4.5

Mercy and Lisa were playing being princesses. They had laid out a roll of blue fabric on the floor.

Mercy: 'Pretend this is river right – you have to get across to find your daddy in the castle.'

Lisa: 'But, but I mustn't mess up my beautiful dress.'

Mercy: 'No, no, pretend you can fly – you have princess magic wings.'

Lisa: 'But, but can I have big wings? I need big wings to fly.'

Mercy: 'Yeh, yeh, fly with big big wings' [she opens her arms and demonstrates]. 'Go up high and you won't fall.'

Comment

The two girls enter an imaginary world where anything is possible. In their play they use language to reflect. They reason:

- if you cross the river you will get wet and spoil your dress
- if you fly across the river your dress will not get wet
- if you have big wings you are better able to fly
- if you fly up high you are less likely to fall.

Screen-based media, home experiences and popular culture

Carrington, in her introduction to Jackie Marsh's book on *Popular Culture*, suggests that we tend to think of young children as inexperienced and innocent who, when entering group settings, need encounters which are linked to familiar issues, to do with their families, homes and pets. This is assumed to build links between their lives at home and in the setting (20). It is counterbalanced by a diet of traditional fairy tales which lead young children into fantasy worlds – we all recognise the enduring popularity of *Cinderella* or *The Gingerbread Man*. I see nothing wrong with this practice unless it ignores other potent influences that children come across at home. These are often not linked to print but rather to television programmes, DVDs and toys (often robotic). The power of the media is such that much of children's play is centred around thinking about and replaying the characters they have viewed. In Case Study 4.4 we see Emily drawing on her interests in three great characters from popular culture – Mickey Mouse and Punch and Judy. While first-hand experiences continue to be paramount, digital technology can be an important source which forms the stuff of imagination. The National Strategies, when looking at supporting young boys' achievement, stated that 'Images and ideas gleaned from the media are common starting points in boys' play and may involve characters with special powers or weapons' (21).

Disasters and acts of terrorism are now replayed continuously on screen and viewed by young children at home on a daily basis. We know that they play out their experiences in an attempt to make sense, and frequently play, particularly from boys, includes elements of aggression. This rough and tumble play has always existed and boys blend their understandings of reality with flights of imagination as they vigorously replay their versions of super-heroes, goodies and baddies.

Writing in *Nursery World*, Weinstein suggests that super-hero play is particularly noticeable in four and five year olds. At this age children want to be strong and powerful, and by taking on superpowers they imagine what might be and acquire courage to overcome their fears (22). Paley reminds us so well of the protection that fantasy affords: 'Fantasy of course is the first line of defence against every sort of fear and in fantasy play the children discover the value of peer support as they dare to face and put the beanstalk to the test' (23).

If, as studies show (24, 25), children are encountering, thinking about and interested in popular media culture at home, then practitioners should build on these experiences in the interests of continuity and to encourage them to engage with a broad range of texts.

Making creative connections

Young children's drive to play around with and connect ideas is summarised so well in the National Strategies document *Learning, Playing and Interacting*.

> Children have 'built-in' exploratory tendencies, and engage all their senses to investigate and master tools and resources, to develop their skills, and to build their knowledge and understanding of the world. The freedom to combine resources in many different ways may be especially important for flexible cognitive development, by enabling children to build pathways for thinking and learning, and to make connections across areas of experience. (26)

Children's creative thinking is a way of generating ideas by re-enacting or re-presenting what they have experienced or imagined in original ways – original, that is, for the child. Other people may have thought of this idea before but it is the child's own discovery.

Sue Robson distinguishes between creative thinking and creativity and suggests that while creative thinking is a part of creativity, it is not the same (27). This is echoed by Anna Craft, who differentiates between the two references to creativity in the EYFS (28). Creative Development (now called *Expressive Arts and Design*) is included as one of the seven areas of Learning and Development; it is recognised in different aspects of the arts, including music, drama, role play, drawing, painting and modelling. Craft terms this 'big C' creativity. Creativity and Critical Thinking (now revised as a learning characteristic *Creating and Thinking Critically*) she defines as 'everyday creativity' – the way in which we imagine, use our ingenuity consider options and make connections to come up with new and creative ideas. Craft terms this 'little c' creativity (29). When young children have the opportunity to practise and apply 'little c' creativity in their day-to-day lives, over time this allows them to alter and deepen their understandings and they make genuine intellectual progress.

Developing creative new thoughts and ideas rarely happens in a 'eureka' moment. Graham Wallas (quoted in Storr) came up with one of the earliest definitions of creative thinking. He suggested that there are several processes involved, namely: preparation, incubation, illumination and verification (30). These are briefly examined below with reference to young children.

Preparation is dependent on children having rich and interesting experiences, exploring and using different materials and having adults available to encourage their investigations. Tina Bruce states that 'play supports the possibility for creative ideas and thoughts to develop. The processes of representation support children's creations' (31).

Incubation involves taking a break, mulling things over and allowing half-formed ideas to strengthen. Claxton suggests that reverie and serendipity are critical to the creative mind. In his book *Hare Brain, Tortoise Mind*, Claxton argues strongly for slower ways of learning to be properly valued. As well as being mentally busy, paying attention to intuition, day dreaming and cogitating can allow understanding to emerge seemingly without effort (32). Many young children lead busy lives filled with activities and the media and have little time to allow ideas to simmer. Susan Linn, an articulate critic of the media onslaught on young children, argues for time and space for incubating ideas:

> Harry Potter did not evolve from a lifetime of exposure to television, movies and the products they sell. His roots are in the silence J.K. Rowling found in the Forest of Dean. He grew in the space she was allowed to fill with her own vision. He grew in the glorious experience – endangered now more than ever – of listening to voices no one else had heard. (33)

So taking a break is critical to allow thoughts to form, but these periods of rest are most effective if they are alternated with times of intense and focused mental and physical activity. Without the activity there is nothing to incubate. We see children deeply engaged and then pausing in their play – they create their own pace to think.

Illumination is when thoughts and ideas which are half-formed start to crystallise and a connection is made. Bruce describes it as having a moment of insight (34).

Verification. Once a new idea is formed, there is a need to ensure that it's valid – to check it out, share it with others.

Case Study 4.2 about Elise illustrates clearly the different processes in her thinking.

- Her interest was captured by the notion of God as the Trinity (this **prepared** her to spend time and energy to make sense of the proposition).
- She had uninterrupted time at home to contemplate and mull over the notion (her thoughts were **incubating** and were as yet unformed).
- She related God as the Trinity to her own family circumstances. Gopnik says that we use what we know to make connections with what we don't know (35). These connections led Elise to **illuminate** or come to a new understanding about the religious precept.
- Having made the connection, Elise needed to communicate it to her teacher to check out or **verify** that her new thinking was sound.

Experienced practitioners recognise that although these four processes contribute to creative thinking, connections are not always formed, and some will emerge and then wither away, but children's other connections are strong. It is the strong connections that give birth to new ideas.

Practical Activity

Observe your key children in bouts of self-chosen play:

- Consider the scope offered for them to develop the four processes of creative thinking.
- Try to identify moments in play when a child incubates, illuminates and verifies a creative thought.

These observations are particularly enlightening if they are shared with a colleague.

Moving, making and marking

Young children continue to represent their understandings of experiences using all means that are made available for them. They will move and dance spontaneously or, in adult-led sessions, respond to music, reflect the wind outside or play out their responses to the story of 'Snow White'. Gunther Kress studied his own children's ways of making meaning and observed them using:

- recycled and natural materials to make models
- household objects combined with toys to create scenarios which they used to act out narratives
- mark-making tools to re-create their understandings (36).

These observations were of children playing at home. Given the opportunity and available resources, children will naturally signify and record in many different ways. It seems, as Anning and Ring suggest, that children are able to move fluidly from one means of representation to another: 'These are capabilities that many artists spend their working lives trying to recapture' (37).

Graphic representations

Many young children will represent their experiences, thoughts and ideas visually. Early on they simply enjoy encounters with paint, chalk and pencil, and the seemingly magical process of making a mark. In time this early experimentation becomes more deliberate. John Matthews believes that 'Scribbles are products of a systematic investigation, rather than haphazard actions' (38).

The National Strategies stated that once young children recognise that their marks can be symbols to carry meaning, they begin to use marks to make their thinking visible (39). Despite this statement, there is a tendency to consider mark-making or drawing simply as a precursor to children's development as writers and mathematicians. There is undoubtedly a link but it is important to understand the differences. Vygotsky considered drawing, like play, to be a primary symbol system which stands for actions and objects. He contrasts this with writing, which he states is a secondary symbol system which stands for spoken words (40). The act of transcribing in writing is a difficult and demanding task for young children. Here we are concerned with children mark-making or drawing to support their thinking. Anning suggests that 'drawing offers a powerful mode for representing and clarifying one's own thinking' (41).

Young children will draw to demonstrate their understandings, to hold thoughts in their mind and to recall events. They are very interested in their surroundings; babies and infants love labelling familiar features in their homes and while going on a walk. They will later represent them in drawings and, with encouragement, will start to make maps. Early maps show buildings and people and other features as elevations rather than as a plan. Essentially, young children's maps emphasise what is important to them – the dog in a map of their bedroom, a pond in their granny's garden.

Case Study 4.6

Figure 4.1

Ross was fascinated by the story of *Rosie's Walk* (Pat Hutchins). His teacher had read the book to the class on several occasions. In small groups, children had used blocks and other open-ended materials to construct Rosie's route and had re-enacted the sequence of the story. Ross enjoyed mark-making, particularly drawing. Recently he had drawn a route showing his journey to school in meticulous detail.

Ross worked on drawing his map of Rosie's walk over two days, talking through aspects of the story as he did so, but without referring to the picture book. On completion, Daisy, his teacher, suggested that they photocopy the drawing so that every child could have a copy to use if they wished to play through the story again. One copy was also attached to the book and this enthused other children to create their own maps.

Comment

Ross's map (see Figure 4.1) shows his understanding of the story, the individual characters involved and his sense of place. He draws from memory, rehearsing the sequence of events in his mind as he commits them to paper. His teacher affirmed Ross's drawing by photocopying the work and followed up the children's interest in maps by sharing and displaying commercial maps and architectural plans. Ross continued his interest in mapmaking by drawing the Wolf's route when he visited the houses of the *Three Little Pigs*.

Making-meaning in early writing

When children start to try out letter shapes they weave them into their drawings, recognising no difference between the two methods. Dyson (quoted in Anning and Ring) states that trying too early to separate drawing and writing detracts from young children's ability to create stories. At this stage, writing appears to supplement the main symbol system of drawing (42). Young children's drawing and writing is fed by what they experience and, in particular, those experiences that really matter to them. They become particularly interested in the letters in their name and the names of people who are close to them as well as labels in environmental print and words in well-loved stories. These will stay in their minds and some will be replayed. The replay may include a brief caption or written message which will emerge from scribbles and drawings.

Figure 4.2

Five year-old Ruby was fascinated by Moby, her grandma's cat. She particularly loved his furry coat, which is the main feature in her drawing. Ruby's writing includes her name and the name of the cat.

Early mathematical thinking

We have seen that many young children's schema are mathematical, for example, showing interests in positioning, enclosing and transporting, which link into aspects of Mathematics described in the new Statutory Framework for the Early Years Foundation Stage (43).

   This section on early mathematical thinking is brief and readers will gain deeper insights from two excellent publications, *Mark Making Matters* and *Children Thinking Mathematically* (44, 45). Most of the following points draw on these documents.

Mathematical graphics
Worthington and Carruthers, who make a major contribution to *Mark Making Matters*, use this term to describe young children's marks as they explore their early thinking.

> Children choose to use their own mathematical graphics to represent their mathematical thinking; in a sense they are thinking on paper. Children, when given the opportunity, will choose to make mathematical marks which can include scribbles, drawing, writing, tallies, invented and standard symbols. Just as in children's early writing, there is also a development in children's early mathematical marks. (46)

Worthington and Carruthers chart the development of mathematical graphics from children's earliest play explorations leading to their own written methods of calculation:

> There is an important distinction between recording mathematics and mathematical graphics. Young children will record a piece of maths after they have completed the mathematics as opposed to children representing their mathematical thinking in contexts which are relevant to them. (47)

Around 3–4 years, children begin to give mathematical meanings to some of their graphics using their marks as symbols to think about quantities and numbers. They use their marks flexibly to represent meanings for different purposes.

Counting skills
Young children are fascinated by numbers and boys in particular like large numbers. Most children are interested in personal numbers (their age, their house number). Given different exposure to numbers, nursery-age children will:

- start to understand one-to-one correspondence
- count numbers in the same order
- recognise that the last number in a count represents the size of the group

- know that they can recognise (subitise) a small number of objects without counting them
- move from counting to calculating, understanding that amounts can be 'added' together or separated by 'taking away'.

Understanding about shape, space and measures

This springs from early sensory encounters with objects and their surroundings. Young children will use their own terms to describe these experiences; importantly, this is what makes sense to them rather than trying to recall the 'correct' name. Their understanding of measurement develops through noting the sequence, pattern and pace of daily routines and when investigating different lengths of fabrics and filling different size containers (48).

Young children initially develop their understandings about their surroundings through first-hand investigation. They recognise position and space as they play. A five year old playing with small-scale animals in a farm-yard setting may space out the animals and then explain that this is to give each one 'room to eat lots of grass'. Children will find room for movement and dance in a large hall and understand the notion of finding a 'space'.

Early thinking about Understanding The World

This revised area of learning in the Statutory Framework for the EYFS is very wide and there is only space to mention young children's thinking about scientific processes which are highlighted in *Understanding The World*.

Some expectations for three and four year olds are for them to:

- know about similarities and differences in relation to places, objects, materials and living things
- make observations of animals and plants and explain why some things occur
- talk about changes, including in simple experiments (49).

Because of their insatiable curiosity, young children are open to all types of science-related encounters. Once again, their early experiences will influence their understandings. One example is their grasp of difference between living and non-living things. Carey found that many four year olds had difficulty in naming any objects that are not alive and such items as tables and clocks were considered alive because they can be associated with movement (50). Changes in such beliefs are not necessarily systematic but will occur as a result of new experiences and in discussion with others. Susan Isaacs, head teacher of the Malting House School in the 1920s, placed great emphasis on children exploring, observing and coming to conclusions in developing their thinking and understanding. This is exemplified in Case Study 4.7, which comprises an extract adapted from her book, quoted by Robson and further adapted in this book (51).

Case Study 4.7 (from the Malting House School)

A rabbit had died in the night at the school.

> *Child*: 'My daddy says that if we put in into water it will get alive again.'
> *Isaacs*: 'Shall we do so and see?'

The children put the rabbit in a bath of water and hypothesise about it, suggesting that movement means it is alive, and discussing floating and sinking as indications of life and death: 'If it floats it's dead, and if it sinks, it's alive.'

They decide that it's dead and all help to bury the rabbit.

The following day two children talk of digging the rabbit up, and suggest that it might not be there because it will have 'gone up to the sky'.

> *Isaacs*: 'Shall we see if it's there?'
> *Isaacs*: 'They found the rabbit and were very interested to see it still there.'

My comment

The children were fascinated by the dead rabbit and used acquired knowledge in experimenting to revive it. They observed reactions from the animal carefully and came up with an explanation of why they knew that the rabbit was dead. They shared views about what might have happened to the rabbit after its burial and tested these out. The children's considered and sustained thinking was charged by a high level of interest and took place in a social context.

Communicating thoughts through talk

In previous sections we have seen how young children convey their understandings in many different ways. This is described so beautifully in the title *The Hundred Languages of Children*, which describes the work of the pre-primary schools in Reggio Emilia (52). However, children's thinking will be strengthened by their ability to express their thoughts and ideas in words. Once they can talk, it helps them to make their higher-level thinking more visible, precise and explicit. Their ability to be fluent talkers will have been created by many exchanges with interested adults and children, close family members and their special person in their setting or school (see Chapter 5).

Vygotsky emphasises that language development helps thinking but equally thought fosters language. He explains this two-way connection by suggesting that although language begins in social interactions, when used as a means of reflection it becomes a tool for thinking (53).

Nigel Hall highlights the critical role of talk, pointing out that because children under five use talk to communicate rather than writing, it is this talk that gives us access to their thinking (54).

By around three years, young children have a wide receptive language and a working stock of words. They start to use markers to highlight an important event or a personal viewpoint (*well*, *like*). Children in the reception year are starting to use language to analyse, enquire, explain, examine, argue and hypothesise. They talk to recall, reflect and re-order their experiences.

Children's conversations with others are usually for a purpose, to gain information, to share things of interest or to achieve something that they want. Tizard and Hughes vividly describe the rich and easy conversations that can take place between four year old girls and their family members within daily routines in the intimacy of their homes. Children learn a whole range of social skills when they observe and imitate others listening, discussing, arguing, bargaining, manipulating and agreeing (55).

Young children ask **questions** endlessly in their search to know and understand more. Practitioners report that three and four year olds commonly ask questions to:

- clarify routines ('what happens next?', 'when is it time to go home?')
- ask permission ('can we go outside now?', 'can we build a den here?')
- find out about their environment ('where are the pencils?')
- help solve a problem ('how does this stick together?')
- explore their anxieties about change ('when are you coming back?', 'who is our new teacher?')
- enquire about something that interests them ('is that shell heavy for the snail to carry?', 'how does the sea go in and out?')
- reflect about puzzling issues ('when will I be old?', 'where is my dead grandma now?', 'can magic help people to be good?').

Some of these questions are simply functional while others show children grappling with really difficult topics.

Tizard and Hughes's study shows that children not only asked questions but returned to them again and again in order to understand more. The authors described this persistence as intellectual search:

> The children in this study seemed in some sense aware that their conceptual framework was not yet substantial enough to cope with their experiences, and engaged themselves actively in the process of improving their intellectual scaffolding. The passages of intellectual search seemed particularly useful in this process, and indicated that the children were at some level aware that protracted dialogue with adults was a useful way of developing their conceptual knowledge. (56)

Case Study 4.8

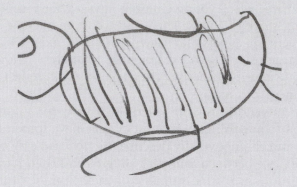

Figure 4.3

Our Dead Fish

A group of three year old nursery children reflect on the death of one of their tropical fish. They discuss how it might have died and then what happens to dead things. One child suggests that it goes to heaven:

Becky (their teacher): 'Where is heaven?'
Kai: 'Down the toilet, that's where heaven is.'
Billy: 'It's up in the sky.'
Eve: 'Heaven is at home.'
Molly B: 'It's in a castle.'
Becky: 'Kai, tell us about heaven down the toilet.'
Kai: 'Through the pipes down the drain underground in water. Cats don't go to the toilet, they go to a different heaven.'
Lewis: 'My dad killed some crabs and ate them. The crabs were sad, they were dead in the sea.'
Billy: 'The fish will go to heaven by itself.'
Katie: 'Down the street, you wait a couple of years, we put the flowers on granddad's grave.'
Becky: 'Down the street?'
Katie: 'Well, near the place, opposite dancing, next door to dancing, we put flowers on.'
Becky: 'At the church?'
Katie: 'Yes, the church. We see him round the corner.'
Becky: 'Do you actually see granddad when you go there?'
Katie: 'I see him in the picture at heaven.'
Becky: 'Why do you put flowers on granddad's grave?'
Katie: 'That's how you do it right? And other granddad's brother is there, and his sister, and other granddad and granddad's other brother. … *They're all there!*'

> **Comment**
>
> Becky very sensitively steers this impressive example of sustained, shared thinking. She is genuinely interested in the conversation and her questions encourage the children to offer freely their ideas about death, heaven, churches, drains and graveyards and their reflections about how and why things happen (57).

Intentional thinking

Young children are not dependent on adults overseeing their efforts or offering them extrinsic rewards. Instead, faced with a problem, they will attempt to solve it and even work towards improvement, having successfully achieved their initial goal. Children progress their thinking in this way. In Karmiloff-Smith's study in the late 1970s, she describes a group of children aged 4–7 attempting to construct a continuous railway circuit for a toy train, using both straight and curved segments of railway line. There is a clear sequence in the way the children attempted the task. The youngest children worked at random and, when the pieces did not fit together, they attempted to make them by use of brute force. The second stage is that of local correction, when children removed the last piece of the track and adjusted it but ignored the rest of the construction. In the third stage, the children started again from scratch, even though parts of the assembly were correct and could have remained. Finally, the oldest and more mature children viewed the construction as a whole and made necessary adjustments to achieve success (58). When this study was repeated, some of the children were determined to improve their construction. Having built the system successfully, they dismantled it and built a new version, pointing out that there were several possible designs (59). These two studies suggest that children progress from using trial and error, and partial correction, to being able to view the totality of the problem. They were learning from their mistakes and from successes and were sensitive to alternative solutions.

Although we can glimpse intentional behaviour in babies and infants (Chapter 3), many of a very young child's actions are initially impulsive and based on 'suck it and see'. It's common for a two year old to choose to engage in an activity – say paint – but then flit to other areas in the nursery. The 'hit and run' approach is quite appropriate at this stage when the child wants to sample as many experiences as she can. Over time the child's approach becomes more purposeful and calculated. Young children progress in their thinking by moving from *ad hoc* choosing to more deliberate planning. By around five years, and with encouragement, children start to have an end point in mind; they select the materials and tools they need, decide where they will work, consider the effects of their actions. Similarly, when children recall experiences and actions they are simply drawing on their working memories. When they move on to reflect any recall is elaborated – they start to become aware of what they have learned, what was interesting and what they can do to extend or build on the experience. Ann Epstein suggests that 'reflection consolidates knowledge so it can be generalised to other situations, thereby leading to further prediction and evaluation' (60).

This intentional behaviour is to do with children taking control or deliberately regulating how they approach and work through a task. Research suggests that all aspects of young children's self-regulation are closely linked to their achievements, regardless of their intelligence. Particularly important are aspects of thinking such as planning and problem solving and emotional aspects, which include resisting impulses, delaying gratification and recognising the consequences of their actions (61). Metacognition or the ability to recognise and think about one's thinking is often closely aligned to self-regulation and sometimes the terms are used interchangeably. Sue Robson usefully suggests that one possible way to distinguish between the two is as follows:

- self-regulation is not constant – a child can choose to adopt the behaviours described above and so regulate her behaviour
- metacognition is more stable – once a child is aware of the ways in which she thinks it is difficult to ignore (62).

However, my observations indicate that both self-regulation and metacognitive behaviours can break down when young children experience stress and anxiety; this often results in regression to impulsive activity.

The Tickell Review acknowledged the importance of self-regulation for young children's all-round development. Tickell recognised that all aspects of self-regulation are highly sensitive to experience and can be enhanced by effective provision in early years settings. In summary, self-regulation is very visible.

It is identified within the prime areas, particularly in personal, social and emotional development (for example, controlling one's own behaviours, managing emotions, negotiating and planning with others) and communication and language (for example, using talk to support thinking, giving reasons and explanations). Other aspects of self-regulation are included within the characteristics of effective learning, which focus on how, rather than what, children learn (63).

One aspect of a self-regulated approach is when children engage in what's termed 'private speech'. They talk to themselves about what they are going to do and how they are going to do it. Studies have found that this is most evident in children's own play where adults were not involved (64, 65).

When we consider how children learn to become self-regulated, there is now good evidence that the best contexts are in children's self-selected play (66). The clear message appears to be that the more that children are controlled and regulated, the less scope there is for them to regulate themselves.

Main messages in this chapter

- Young children's self-esteem and motivation to think is shaped in relationships with those close to them.
- They make sense through enriching and extending their schemes of thinking, and by representing their understandings in fantasy play, when moving, making things and mark-making.
- These essential early experiences help to secure basic concepts.
- Children connect past experiences to new encounters and so create fresh thoughts and ideas.
- Using spoken language, they begin to make complex thoughts more precise and explicit.
- Children learn to regulate their behaviour and use and apply their thoughts more deliberately, particularly in episodes of self-chosen play.

References

1. Bodrova, E. and Leong, D.J. (2008) 'Developing Self-regulation in Kindergarten: Can We Keep All the Crickets in the Basket?', *Beyond the Journal: Young Children on the Web*, March. Washington, DC: National Association for the Education of Young Children, p. 1.
2. Tickell, C. (2011) *The Early Years: Foundations for Life, Health and Learning*. An Independent Report to HM Government on the Early Years Foundation Stage. London: Department for Education.
3. Bodrova and Leong (2008) 'Developing Self-regulation in Kindergarten' (see note 1), p. 2.
4. Siegler, R., DeLoache, J. and Eisenberg, N. (2003) *How Children Develop*. New York: Worth, p. 428.
5. Dweck, C. (1988) 'A Socio-cognitive Approach to Motivation and Achievement', *Psychological Review*, 95(2): 256–73.
6. Duckworth, A., Matthews, M. and Kelly, D. (2007) 'Grit, Perseverance and Passion for Long-term Goals', *Journal of Personality and Social Psychology*, 92(6): 1087–101.
7. Dweck, C. (2006) *Mind-set: The New Psychology of Success*. New York: Random House.
8. Carr, M. and Claxton, G. (2002) 'Tracking the Development of Learning Dispositions', *Assessment in Education*, 9: 19–37.

9. Carr, M. and Claxton, G. (2004) 'A Framework for Teaching Learning: The Dynamics of Dispositions', *Early Years*, 24 January, pp. 87–96.

10. Laevers, F. (2005) *Wellbeing and Involvement in Care: A Process-Oriented Self-Evaluation Instrument for Care Settings*. Flanders: Belgium, Leuven University Research Centre for Experiential Education.

11. Evangalou, M., Sylva, K. and Kyriacou, M. (2009) *Early Years Learning and Development Literature Review*. London: Department for Children, Schools and Family (DCSF), p. 78.

12. Dunn, J. (2004) *Children's Friendships*. Oxford: Blackwells.

13. Vygotsky, L. (1978) *Mind in Society*. Cambridge, MA: Harvard University Press.

14. Arnold, C. (1990) quoted in T. Bruce (1997) *Early Childhood Education*. London: Hodder & Stoughton, p. 81.

15. Meadows, S. (1993) *The Child as Thinker*. London: Routledge, p. 111.

16. Verrier, N. (2000) 'Nursery School Event Representation and Organisation: A Longitudinal Study in Young French Children', *European Journal of Psychology of Education*, XV(3): 313–28.

17. Fernyhough, C. (2008) *The Baby in the Mirror: A Child's World from Birth to Three*. London: Granta Books, p. 169.

18. Evangalou et al. (2009) *Early Years Learning and Development Literature Review* (see note 11), p. 78.

19. Paley, V.G. (2004) *A Child's Work: The Importance of Fantasy Play*. Chicago, IL and London: University of Chicago Press, p. 8.

20. Carrington, V. (2005) 'New Textual Landscapes', in J. Marsh (ed.), *Popular Culture, New Media and Digital Literacy in Early Childhood*. Abingdon: Routledge Falmer, p. 21.

21. National Strategies (2007) *Confident, Capable and Creative: Supporting Boys' Achievements*. London: Department for Children, Schools and Family (DCSF), p. 16.

22. Weinstein, N. (2011) 'All about Superhero Play', *Nursery World*, 20 September–3 October, pp. 15–19.

23. Paley, V. (1990) *The Boy Who Would Be a Helicopter*. Chicago, IL: University of Chicago Press, p. 59.

24. Coles, M. and Hall C. (2002) 'Gendered Readings: Learning from Children's Reading Choices', *Journal of Research in Reading*, 25(1): 265–85.

25. Makin, L., Hayden, J., Holland, A., Arthur, L., Beecher, B., Jones, D.C. and McNaught, M. (1999) *Mapping Literacy Practices in Early Childhood Services*. Sydney: NSW Department of Education and Training and NSW Department of Community Services.

26. National Strategies (2009) *Learning, Playing and Interacting*. London: Department for Children, Schools and Family, p. 6.

27. Robson, S. (2006) *Developing Thinking and Understanding in Young Children*. London: Routledge.

28. Department for Education and Skills (2008) *The Early Years Foundation Stage, Principles into Practice Card: 4.4 Creative Development, 4.3 Creativity and Critical Thinking*. London: DfES.

29. Craft, A. (2010) 'Creative Thinking and Creative Development', quoted in Department for Children, Schools and Families (2010) The National Strategies Early Years, *Finding and Exploring Young Children's Fascinations*. London: DCSF, p.13.

30. Storr, A. (1989) *Solitude*. London: HarperCollins, p. 25.
31. Bruce, T. (2006) *Cultivating Creativity in Babies, Toddlers and Young Children*. London: Hodder & Stoughton, p. 21. London: Fourth Estate.
32. Claxton, G. (1997) *Hare Brain, Tortoise Mind*.
33. Linn, S. (2004) 'The Seashore of Endless Worlds', in T. Bruce (ed) *Early Childhood Practice: The Journal for Multi-Professional Partnerships*, 8(1), 2006, p. 60.
34. Bruce (2006) *Cultivating Creativity in Babies, Toddlers and Young Children* (see note 31), p. 23.
35. Gopnik, A. (2009) *The Philosophical Baby*. London: Bodley Head, p. 244.
36. Kress, G. (1997) *Before Writing: Rethinking the Paths to Literacy*. London: Routledge.
37. Anning, A. and Ring, K. (2004) *Making Sense of Children's Drawings*. Maidenhead: Open University Press, p. 3.
38. Matthews, J. (1999) *The Art of Childhood and Adolescence: The Construction of Meaning*. Brighton: Falmer Press, p. 19.
39. Department for Children, Schools and Families (2008) *Mark Making Matters*. London: DCFS, p. 3.
40. Vygotsky (1978) *Mind in Society* (see note 13).
41. Anning, A. (1997) 'Drawing Out Ideas: Graphicacy and Young Children', *International Journal of Technology and Design Education*, 7 (3): pp. 219–39.
42. Anning and Ring (2004) *Making Sense of Children's Drawings* (see note 37), p. 5.
43. Department for Education (2012) *Statutory Framework for the Early Years Foundation Stage*. London: DfE.
44. Department for Children, Schools and Families (2008) *Mark Making Matters* (see note 39).
45. Department for Children, Schools and Families (2009) *Children Thinking Mathematically: Problem Solving, Reasoning and Numeracy in the EYFS*. London: DfCFS.
46. Department for Children, Schools and Families (2008) *Mark Making Matters* (see note 39), p. 34.
47. Department for Children, Schools and Families (2009) *Children Thinking Mathematically* (see note 45), p. 15.
48. Ibid., pp. 32–7.
49. Department for Education (2012) *The Statutory Framework for the EYFS*. London: DfE, 4.
50. Carey, S. (1985) *Conceptual Change in Childhood*. Boston, MA: MIT Press/ Bradford Books.
51. Isaacs, S. (1930) 'Intellectual Growth in Young Children', in S. Robson (1996), *Developing Thinking and Understanding in Young Children*. Abingdon: Routledge, p. 91.
52. Edwards, C., Gandini, L. and Forman, G. (1993) *The Hundred Languages of Children: The Reggio Emilia Approach to Early Childhood Education*. Norwood, NJ: Ablex.
53. Vygotsky (1978) *Mind in Society* (see note 13).
54. Hall, N. (1996) *Listening to Children Think*. London: Hodder & Stoughton, p. v.
55. Tizard, B. and Hughes, M. (2002) *Young Children Learning: Talking and Thinking at Home and at School* (2nd edn). London: Fontana.

56. Ibid., pp. 105–6.
57. Wingate Nursery School, extract from *Our Dead Fish: Young Children Exploring the Ideas of Life and Death, Heaven and Earth.* Email: wingatetrainingbase@durhamlearning.net.
58. Karmiloff-Smith, A. (1979) 'Problem Solving Construction and Representations of Closed Railway Circuits', *Archives of Psychology*, 47: 37–59.
59. Deloache, J.S. and Brown, A.L. (1987) 'The Early Emergence of Planning Skills in Children', in J. Bruner and H. Haste (eds), *Making Sense*. London: Methuen.
60. Epstein, A. (2003) 'How Planning and Reflection Develop Young Children's Thinking Skills', *Beyond the Journal: Young Children on the Web*, September, p. 3.
61. Bodrova and Leong (2008) 'Developing Self-regulation in Kindergarten' (see note 1).
62. Robson (2006) *Developing Thinking and Understanding in Young Children* (see note 27), p. 80.
63. Tickell (2011) *The Early Years* (see note 2), p. 87.
64. Berk, L. (2008), quoted in article by Alex Spiegel, 'Old-fashioned Play Builds Serious Skills', on National Public Radio, 21 April, www.npr.org/templates/story/story.php?storyId=19212514
65. Kuvalja, M. (2009) 'Private Speech, Play and Self-regulation', quoted in David Whitebread (2009) *Play and Self-regulation in Young Children*, European Association for Research on Learning and Instruction (EARLI) Conference, Amsterdam, August.
66. McEntire, N. (2009) 'Creative Play Increases Children's Self-regulation: A Convergence of Clinical and Educational Considerations', *Childhood Education*, 85(3), Spring: 210.

5

How Close Adults can Support Young Children's Thinking at 3–5 Years

Intentions

This chapter:

- recognises how developing relationships with special people and their friends help young children to think in a social context
- considers how close adults:
  - o enable a smooth and positive transition into the reception class
  - o support young children's thinking and communication through talk
  - o help them to make sense
  - o provide conditions to aid self-regulation and metacognition

Twenty years ago John Brierley summed up the critical brain development that takes place in the early years of life and the implications for work with young children:

> During these years of swift brain growth a child's eyes, ears and touch sense in particular are absorbing experiences of all kinds through imitation and exploration. It is obvious that the quality of experience is vital for sound development. (1)

Building on sound very early foundations, children in the early years settings have everything going for them as their personalities blossom and flourish and their powers of intellectual search strengthen. Working with children of 3–5 years demands stamina (intellectual, emotional and physical) and commitment but the rewards are great.

Relationships

As children move through the EYFS their need for close attachments with special people is as strong as ever and friendships now play an important part. The key to children's social understandings is founded on their relationships with close adults; they also develop their thinking with other children.

The special person plays a key role in helping a child become a master thinker and learner and adopt the positive learning dispositions indicated in the previous chapter. Effective practices include the following:

Knowing the child

A strong relationship is based on knowing each child intimately and so recognising how she or he ticks. Within a group setting, every child needs to know that she is known and practitioners go to great lengths to show this as part of their everyday practice.

- Home visits are expensive of time but are of immense value for all parties involved and a wonderful opportunity for a child to establish a personal link with her special person. This is often shown when the child meets the practitioner later in the setting and bursts forth with delighted responses such as: *'You came to my house, you saw my toys, will you come again?'* When Jacqui Cousins asked some four year olds for their reactions to the home visit from their teacher the very strong message was that it was hugely valued. The children expected that the teacher was coming to meet them, to see their toys and share their interests. Where this did not happen because the teacher was more involved in admission forms, the children were sadly disappointed (2).
- Daily greetings will include personalised comments and questions such as: *'Hello Dylan – how's that new puppy?'*, *'Oh I like your smart new shoes Annie'*, *'Has your mum had the baby yet Marcus?'* These natural greetings demonstrate to each of these children that their special person remembers and is interested in things that matter to them.

> ### Professional checkpoint
>
> How can I be sure that every child knows that I know them?

Observing and listening

Julian Grenier's guidance in the Social and Emotions Aspects of Development (SEAD) document suggests that deep knowledge and understanding of individual children comes from spending time with your key group at play, good information sharing with parents and close and regular observation (3).

Wise practitioners know that nothing can take the place of being alongside the child at different times of the day, noting his responses to experiences and listening to conversations.

Being observant of children is at the heart of practice. The rationale behind observational based assessment is that, unless you know what children enjoy doing, and what they know and understand, it is not possible to pitch experiences at their level or to provide appropriate resources and interventions to challenge them further. Moreover, in order to find out what children are thinking, practitioners must observe and listen and then take an imaginative leap into the child's mind.

Observation involves watching with perception and ways of looking informed by knowledge of child development. When practitioners plan time to regularly observe in this way, their eyes are opened to the unique characteristics and talents of each baby and young child.

Although good practitioners have been observing children for years, it is increasingly clear that it doesn't always come easily and naturally. Observation is a complex skill which is honed with experience. It is too easy to look and not see or listen and not hear and so miss critical moments of development and thinking. The more we learn about observing in depth and the longer we observe children, so our knowledge and understanding builds up and becomes internalised in our professional repertoire.

There are several ways of making observations. Some should be planned, but experienced practitioners are also vigilant to capture at any time spontaneous but important responses from children during the course of the day. Practitioners may also gain valuable insights when they participate in play.

Case Study 5.1

Bimla and Daisy (four years) were playing with small world resources. Bimla called to Janice, her key person. 'Janice, will you help us?' Janice cheerfully agreed and asks the two girls what is happening.

Bimla: 'You see, Janice, little teddy is going to big school and he's frightened, he's really frightened.'

Daisy: 'Yeh an, an he doesn't want to go, does he Bimla, so he shuts himself in this box' [squeezes the bear into a small box] 'oh no he won't fit'.

Bimla: 'His mummy is looking for him' (uses a high pitched voice) 'Teddy, Teddy where are you, come on Teddy.'

(Continued)

(Continued)

> Daisy: 'Shhh… he is hiding from his mum cos he doesn't like big school. It's … its too big and the children are big, so Ted won't go'.
>
> Bimla: 'But his mummy is cross, Janice, what will happen?'
>
> Janice: 'Poor Teddy, I think that we need to help him and then he might start to like school. Perhaps we might find him a friend.'

Comment

Janice listened carefully to the graphic drama. She quickly realised that the two girls were playing out their own fears about moving to the reception class the following term. Having been invited to join the play, Janice was able to immediately suggest ways to help Ted, which she hoped would allay some of their anxiety.

Underpinning successful observation is a desire to know about key children. For each new entrant, practitioners will ask two questions. 'What sort of a child is this' – and then, 'how do I know?'

Observations of child-initiated play

Successful assessments and judgements about young children are founded on observations of their learning and behaviour. These moments are most evident when children are engaged in play and selecting their own activities. Guidance in the handbook from the Qualifications and Curriculum Development Agency suggests that, when gaining evidence of children learning, no more than 20% of observations should take place in adult-directed activity. The vast majority of information about children will be gathered in child-chosen activities (4). This sensible guidance is given for two reasons:

- We can only find out so much about a child if we direct an activity. At the sticking table where children in turn are required to assemble pre-cut shapes onto paper, practitioners will find out if they can apply glue and maybe if they have developed a notion of pattern. In a directed maths activity using, for example, small plastic bears, we are likely to find out about children's understanding of relative size and whether they are able or prepared to concentrate on this activity. Now contrast this with the array of information we might gather when children make their own decisions about their experiences: What do they select? How do they set about the activity? If it's a shared enterprise, how do they negotiate with others? What previous experience do they bring to the activity? A little boy gazing into a saucepan of pretend soup he is stirring in a role-play area mutters '*Now* who is the fairest of us all'; surely he knows something of the story of 'Snow White' and makes a connection with his cooking activity.

- When a child demonstrates a skill or ability in a directed activity, this is still a fragile level of understanding. Only when his new learning is applied in self-directed activity or play do we know that it has been assimilated and is secure.

When the special person knows her children intimately, this richly informs what she makes of her observations. She understands that Titus keeps injecting the dolls with a pretend syringe as he recalls and plays through the traumas of a recent stay in hospital. She recognises why Skyla is energetic and full of ideas, knowing that this little girl, who lives in a tiny flat, is in her element playing freely outside.

Grenier states the direct benefits of knowing children intimately:

> Learning what your key children's conversations, play and behaviour mean will enable you to better understand the connections they are making in their learning and to engage in sustained shared thinking. (5)

However, the joyful and seemingly natural inclination to play is not obvious in all children, particularly if they have experienced abuse and trauma. In these cases, the adult plays a critical role as a co-player, both playing alongside the child, helping them to adopt a character role and turn-take, and then gently encouraging the child to play with others.

Extending relationships with close others

By 3–4 years, most children's passions for playing with other children 'has taken off at an astonishing trajectory' (6). Practitioners recognise continuous questions from children seeking affirmation of friendship: 'You're my friend, aren't you?', or a heartrending cry of 'Ibu won't play with me'.

Friendship pairs seem to be more successful in solving problems than non-friendship groups. This seems due to friends being prepared to discuss and reflect on their solutions together (7). Because friendships matter so much, practitioners will ensure that young children develop interpersonal skills and attitudes to help them rub along with others.

Children fall in and out of friendships. Until they learn to see another's perspective and to express their feelings and thoughts in words, they will use physical action to protect their rights. McTavish suggests that learning simple techniques of conflict resolution will help. These involve the adult:

- asking each child to describe or show what happened and to listen carefully to the other's point of view
- helping them to recognise and reflect back what has caused the anger to erupt for each child. For example, 'You are really cross Ilsa because Megan pushed you and took the red bike you were waiting for. You are angry Megan because you had been waiting a long time for the bike and when you took it Alma punched you hard.'
- encouraging children to suggest what they could do now to make things better
- discussing options with them in order to decide on the best suggestion.

Requiring children to say sorry is not helpful; the sentiment is often meaningless to a young child and McTavish suggests that it can detract from the conflict (8).

Sometimes, however, we can be too hasty in rushing in to help. The delightful film clip from Siren Films, showing two three year olds playing together, reveals how capable and creative they can be in thinking how to mend arguments and maintain friendships (9).

Friendships really help young children's well-being and also support their cognitive development. Broadhead backs this when she notes in her study that the more co-operative the children's play theme, the more likely they are to recognise and appreciate the thoughts and perspectives of their friends (10). Children as young as five can accept that others have beliefs different from their own, although they were less tolerant in their judgements than older children (11). Robson summarises the significance of relationships: 'There seem good reasons to conclude that shared experiences are a key part of children's development as thinkers' (12).

In order to support children's friendships practitioners may:

- provide a new child with a friend who can help to explain routines and show the new entrant resources to play with
- encourage a more mature child to explain/show a less mature child how to do something
- include many opportunities for turn-taking and sharing
- sharing stories which show examples of empathy
- encourage children to share interests, by encouraging those who have a common schema to play together
- allow children initially to resolve conflicts in their own way.

Links with Parents

Listen carefully to parents' accounts of their children's friendships at home and note if and how they differ from the child's social relationships in the setting/school.

Relationships with parents and children

When young children see the people who matter to them most, their parents and special persons, engaged in open and trusting relationships, their emotional security is secured. One valuable spin-off of a strong, shared relationship is that parents and practitioners develop a shared understanding of and interest in the child's preoccupations or schema.

Sharing understandings about children's schema

Parents are always well disposed towards their children and have really valuable insights into their personalities. Despite this, they do not always recognise the thinking which lies behind their young children's comments and ideas. Practitioners can both gain from parents' knowledge and also help them to have insights into their children's minds. Chris Athey's Froebel Early Childhood Project encouraged practitioners to share their professional knowledge with parents about how their children learn and how this is represented through their schema:

> One of the most important outcomes of the project was that all the adults watched and listened with ever increasing interest to what the children were saying and doing. Nothing gets under a parent's skin more quickly and more permanently than the illumination of his or her own children's behaviour. The effect of participation is profound. (13)

Useful work with parents includes:

- taking the mystique out of schema, helping them to recognise that they simply reflect children's deep and abiding interests, usually shown in their play
- offering informal training sessions which give straightforward information about common schemes of thinking
- providing them with video cameras (or they may have smart phones) and asking them to capture examples of their child at play in the home; the clips can then be shared and discussed with a small group of parents and practitioners in order to highlight any particular schemes of thought
- encouraging parents who are already experienced 'schema spotters' to share with the key person how they have provided additional stimulus to enrich the scheme of thought observed
- emphasising that the very best way for parents to tune into their children is by genuinely enjoying their company and sharing lives together.

Links with Parents

How can my home visits help parents to gain insights into supporting their children thinking?

Supporting young children as thinkers during transitions

We are all involved in transitions in life and the major ones (birth dates, marriages, anniversaries) constitute a rite of passage. These times signal an important stage in life, which involve moving on, and they mean change and some disequilibrium. They can cause us to be excited and full of anticipation. Equally, they can create feelings of anxiety, trepidation, uncertainty and fear. Young children will also experience these feelings, the difference being that they have less life experience than adults and can be threatened by change.

Close and supportive relationships are the key to smoothing transition times

It's worrying that many young children can make several transitions during the Foundation Stage at a time when they really need stability. These moves may be from daycare at three years, followed by a nursery setting and then to school. Even within one setting some children move to several different provisions during the course of one day: from breakfast club to morning daycare, followed by core provision in a nursery group and finally to extended care and tea time. Their day may last from 7.00 am to 6.00 pm and involve relating to different adults, and adapting to different contexts, expectations and routines. In order to survive children have to understand about and accommodate to what is often a bewildering number of different adults and environments. This approach does not heed the child's needs and is likened to 'pass the parcel' as a child is handed on to the next type of provision throughout the day.

Until recently, the move from a nursery setting to the reception class entailed tremendous change for young children. However, since the reception year was included in the EYFS, practice has developed, often dramatically. In many cases now, close liaison between practitioners and careful planning provides a child with continuity of experiences but with sufficient challenge to provoke new thinking. Where a transition occurs that is pleasurable and promises new challenges and only requires very minor adjustments, it can actually recharge us. We all learn through new experiences and conversely a diet of 'sameness' can lead to boredom and can restrict development.

Nevertheless, meticulous planning for continuity does not apply everywhere and even in the best circumstances, for some young children the move from nursery into a reception class can be a momentous experience. The Early Years Foundation Stage reminds us that 'Some children and their parents will find transition times stressful while others will enjoy the experience, and every child's learning journey takes a personal path based on their own individual interests, experiences and the curriculum on offer' (14). Moreover, children's mind-sets will impact on their ability to adapt to a new working environment. The child with a fixed mind-set can find the prospect of any change difficult.

When we have negative feelings it can have an effect on our working memory or mental space, which is in fact the number of items the mind can cope with at any one time. Young children can only concentrate and deal with one or two things at once – as they mature, their capacity to juggle with more items increases. Over time, their skills and ideas are assimilated (see Chapter 1) and they do not have to think consciously about how to do them. Most four year olds are quite able to feed themselves, pour a drink and understand how to build and assemble in a construction area that is familiar to them.

Anxiety and worry takes up a great deal of space in working memory, with the result that a person is unable to concentrate and think clearly. If a transition causes a child stress, her anxieties limit her mental competences with the result that she appears distracted and forgetful.

The child's special person will note those children who are distressed and forgetful and understand that they are particularly in need of her time and support. Veronica Read suggests that:

> Children, during the settling in period, rely on their sense perceptions of touch, taste, smell, seeing and their affect to guide them through the first few weeks. Each child is hoping that their class teachers will hold something special about them in mind across weekends and holidays to reassure them as they negotiate sharing their new teacher with thirty others. (15)

Developing attached relationships for practitioners in a large reception class is not easy and there is no one prescription. The following practices will help a child to become familiar with her new class and to feel secure and known as an individual.

- Start transition procedures early in the year so that an attachment between the child and practitioners can grow and the child can assimilate new experiences gradually to store in his working memory.
  - o Make an initial contact early on with a welcome letter to the child from the teacher(s) which has their photograph on the letter heading.
  - o Have regular 'Welcome to School' sessions where the practitioners are play partners and encourage children to explore provision.
  - o Introduce Eric the puppet, who moves into the reception class. Produce an accompanying book with photographs of Eric showing what he experiences during the school day. Include what he needs

to know and do and how he feels. Use Eric during early contacts with children and during the initial weeks settling in to school.

- o Introduce class routines gradually over a period of time and return to them, playing games encouraging children to remember where they will hang their coats and how they can play in different areas of provision.
- o Note when children are interested in particular routines and aspects of play as these are the ones that will be remembered.

- Find out all you can about a child prior to admission.
  - o If possible arrange for teaching assistants to accompany teachers on home visits and visits to pre-school – their early contact with a child is as important as it is for the teacher and their reflections will supplement the teacher's observations.
  - o Listen carefully to the child's previous special person's comments. Conversations often provide valuable additional information to written records and bring the child to life.
  - o In friendly discussion with parents, draw on their knowledge of their child: what does he enjoy doing and talking about at home (interests, schemes of thought, links with wider family)?; what friends does he have?
  - o Refer to this intelligence when building up a relationship with the child and show him that you know about him and are interested in his life.

- Bring the child's home life into the classroom.
  - o Take a photograph (or ask parents to provide one) of the child with a close family member and have this on display on the first day of school.
  - o Ask the child to bring in a photograph of his favourite place in his home or provide a photo of his pet and encourage him to tell you about it (if this is not appropriate, provide him with a camera and encourage him to take an image of a place that he likes in his classroom).

- Be predictable in order to support a child's 'script' of what happens in school.
  - o Always be available in the same place to greet the child and parent in the morning.
  - o Use the same words and gestures to signal what is to happen next.
  - o Display a visual chart which shows the sequence of events during the session and use this to support the child's understanding of the pattern of the day.

- Use additional adults to allow children easy access to an adult during the start to school.
  - o Invite a group of parents who have worked in reception with you previously to join you as voluntary helpers during the initial

weeks of the term. Provide some guidance to help them to be alert to the needs of children at certain times of the day, for example, at arrival times, clearing up, break times and lunchtimes.

- Minimise change during the early days in school.
  - o Allow the children to become familiar and settled in their classroom and outside area before you introduce them to hall times.
  - o Arrange for the child's special person or another close adult from nursery to accompany new children into reception and remain with them during the early days of settling in.

Until a child has made a secure transition to her new setting or class her thinking and learning is arrested.

Communication and companionship

The central idea in the Reggio schools is of the 'rich child who is, on his own initiative, capable of making meaning from experiences' (16). The special person, as the child's thinking companion, will provide the conditions for this by:

- encouraging children to access and select from a broad range of experiences
- supporting and trusting them to use a rich environment
- giving them time to make sense of what they experience
- having her eyes and ears open to the multiplicity of ways in which children can convey their thoughts and understandings
- acknowledging and respecting children's quiet times of absorbed activity
- being responsive to each child's differing need for her special person to be present, attentive and available as a co-player and partner in conversation
- uncovering the child's level of thinking, knowing when to contribute to his ideas and when to allow his mental disequilibrium to build new understandings.

Some of these conditions are explored further in the section on 'Promoting intentional thinking'.

Children need to communicate through talk as fluency is the key to influence. Through using words children can:

- express their needs, thoughts and ideas and begin to have a stake in their own lives
- be social and rub along with others
- say how they feel.

Supporting talk

We have seen how babies and infants are supported by their special person to communicate through gesture and early sounds. By three years, children need help to develop spoken language, which will in turn help close adults to move closer to the child's thinking.

> Our attempts as teachers to get inside children's heads and understand their understandings are enriched to the extent that children themselves are prepared to give us, through their talk, access to their thinking. (17)

If the special person has worked with child previously, she will be aware of his body language, how his talk has developed and special words that he uses to describe events and experiences. Using her intimate knowledge of each child, she will help each individual to become a fluent communicator using language to express thoughts more clearly and precisely.

A powerful way to do this involves having friendly and companionable conversations. Interactions with young children should, above all, stem from an interest in what they are doing and thinking, and should be based on easy exchanges. The ways in which we chat with children should be similar to having a conversation with a good friend and include:

- showing genuine pleasure at the prospect of the child's company
- giving your full attention, having eye contact, smiling, nodding
- affirming, using 'tags' to show your continued interest – 'I know', 'did you really?', 'my goodness', 'I see'
- inviting the child to elaborate – 'I really want to hear about this'
- recapping to help the child to 'stick to his story' – 'So, you think that...'
- clarifying ideas – 'Right Suki, so you think that this cake mixture will get bigger if we cook it'
- using encouragement to further thinking – 'You have really thought hard about where to put this door in the palace, Rob, but where on earth will you put the windows?'
- speculating – 'Do you think that the three bears would have liked Goldilocks to come to live with them as their friend?'
- offering an alternative viewpoint – 'Do you know, I think that when the three bears discovered Goldilocks, they should have called the police'
- reciprocating – 'I like fish and chips like you Kwame. In fact when I went home last night I was too tired to cook supper and I went to your chip shop and bought fish and chips'.

Links with Parents

Encourage parents to have everyday conversations with their child:

- discuss what they need to buy at the supermarket
- plan together where they might go for an outing at the weekend
- ask them for suggestions about what to eat for lunch.

For those parents who are less confident or not inclined to converse:

- share the conversations you have had with their children about everyday events and give examples of the children's interesting responses
- emphasise how easy it is to share a chat and that their children will enjoy it as much as adults do when chatting with a friend.

Questioning

The way in which practitioners use questions and support children's questions profoundly affects children's thinking.

Using open and closed questions

Several years ago we considered the relative merits of asking children 'closed' and 'open' questions. Closed questions, such as 'What shape is it?', were considered limiting as the adult already had one fixed answer in her mind and the child was forced to guess what that was. Open questions, such as 'Why did it happen?' and 'How does it work?', were considered to better support children's thinking as the queries give range to a number of options. Now we recognise that there is a place for both types of question. Open questions are sometimes 'too big and complex'. The child may have put all his efforts into a drawing or model, but is not sufficiently clear in his mind to frame his response in words. Occasionally, a closed question is a way into an open question.

Case Study 5.2

Louis, almost four years, announced that he was going to build a giant trap to catch baddies. He worked in the construction area for most of the session, all the time very focused on combining blocks, planks, ropes, nets and drapes to create his trap. Millie his key person approached him.

Millie: 'Oh, Louis that's wonderful – now how does it work?'

Louis ignored the question and busied himself adding more planks and ropes. Millie bent down to get nearer to the construction.

(Continued)

(Continued)

Millie: 'Louis, I'm really interested in this but I don't know much about traps. I'm guessing but I wonder if this is where the baddies will enter?'

Louis: 'Yes it is and when they go in there they get stuck in this net, so they can't move and they are prisoners.'

Comment

Although Louis initially had a clear plan, his trap had grown organically. After putting all his efforts into 'doing', he was probably not sufficiently clear in his mind to respond to Millie's initial question. Her second question was more manageable and did not put him under pressure. Louis was also reassured that Millie was not an expert on traps but was seeking guidance from him.

Using possibility questions

Anna Craft suggests that problem finding and problem solving are the basis for creative thinking: 'When young children are encouraged to think about what might be, instead of being asked "what is", the sophistication of their thinking is often revealed' (18). Craft describes this as 'possibility thinking' and proposes the following helpful 'possibility questions':

- What does that remind you of?
- What do you think might happen next?
- What do you/don't you like about this? Why?
- Is there another way (do you think)?
- How could…?
- What would you do if…?
- What do you think?

Although possibility questions are similar to open questions, they are more collaborative, encouraging a personal view and suggesting shared thinking on an equal basis.

Supporting young children's questions

In the previous chapter we touched on how children of this age continually ask questions. The practitioner will take these seriously and recognise that children's enquiries will inform how she can support them further. The following actions help children to understand that their questions are important.

- Keep a question book and note down children's questions, in particular those which invite enquiry and reflection. Replay some of these questions in small-group times and invite children to consider and discuss them.
- Ask children if they would like to have their question displayed in the room – draw attention to interesting questions that individuals have asked during the week.

It is also helpful to note the incidence of, and hotspots for, children's questions.

> ## Professional checkpoints
>
> - When and where are children most likely to ask questions?
> - What types of question do they ask?
> - To whom are these questions directed?

Children will not ask questions unless they are inclined to do so or if there is little to ask questions about.

> ## Professional checkpoint
>
> What is there in my room that provokes young children to wonder and want to investigate?

Taking a back seat

This does not involve the practitioner opting out of talk but rather showing companionable attention in small-group discussions. She listens with interest and acknowledges contributions from different children.

Teachers involved in a national project investigating how they might encourage children's talk with each other had valuable insights to offer. One teacher bravely agreed to be filmed having a discussion with children about a well-known story. Having viewed the film clip herself, she reflected that she had learned nothing about the children's thinking or their behaviour, largely because she had not allowed their voices to be heard.

In a second filming sequence, which showed children starting to sustain discussions among themselves, the teacher had carried out the following moves:

- she offered a comment about the story rather than questioning the children
- after she had raised an issue she remained silent and waited for a response
- she stressed to the children that being quiet is thinking time and quite acceptable (19).

Another teacher, wanting her group of three children to respond to each other, tried three strategies:

- to say less and leave more time for children to comment
- to acknowledge each child's contribution with a smile or nod only and then wait
- to look at other children when one of them has said something (20).

Both of these teachers realised that by responding more to children rather than dominating conversations they were allowing children to take more control.

Many further suggestions for developing conversations with children can be found in the former National Strategies programme *Every Child a Talker* (21).

Climate

Support meaning-making

The most important support that close adults can offer young children when they are trying to make and convey sense is to:

- recognise, respect and promote ways for them to represent their understandings
- provide a climate which allows them access to a wide range of resources which they combine, adapt and use to create scenarios.

Support fantasy and pretend play

Fantasy and pretend play is probably at its peak by three years of age. However, some children will appear to be particularly accomplished players; often this can be tracked back to the very early years when they had many opportunities to observe and imitate behaviour and develop their own ideas. Children still need these opportunities and to know that their pretend play is respected and valued.

Practitioners can offer good support by:

- being aware of children's previous play experiences and their favourite play themes
- giving them time, encouragement, space and resources to create different play scenarios
- taking a back seat and trusting children to develop the play.

Nevertheless, although play should not be controlled, it will be enriched with some adult input by:

- introducing rich stimulus for children to weave into their fantasy play
- pump-priming the play if it becomes repetitive and children begin to lose interest
- feeding children's imagination with stories.

Case Study 5.3

A colleague visited a reception class carrying some curled and blackened branches collected from trees nearby. He explained to the children that he had found something mysterious and very rare – these were dragon's claws! The children were entranced; they handled them (some gingerly), smelt them and some drew the claws. In their play later, a group of children introduced a fiery dragon who was very sad because he had lost his claws.

Comment

The adult's 'sparkly thinking' had stimulated some children to weave the dragon's claws into their fantasy play.

Harness thinking derived from screen-based media and popular culture

We are rapidly moving away from disapproving of many children's huge interest in characters and situations they encounter through digital media and comics. At least there is a resigned acceptance of it being inevitable. But if these scenarios absorb children, we must regard them seriously as food for thought.

Practitioners can support super-hero play by:

- becoming familiar with the characters – their traits and exploits: this gives you credibility to engage in conversations about the heroes

- helping to build contexts around the characters – for example, create a home for Ben 10, prepare his favourite meal
- selecting a small library of books that depict intriguing, exciting and fast-moving stories of super-heroes
- having available open-ended resources (ropes, planks, fabrics, stones) to use with small world super-hero figures
- moving outside: Helen Bromley suggests that super-hero play outside allows children more scope to be messy, noisy and active than is possible inside; she suggests creating a super-hero training camp where children can practise the physical skills used by their hero (22)
- agreeing with children the ground rules for acceptable super-hero play: ask them to think carefully about possible rules and discuss them with friends before coming to a common agreement.

Support mark-making

- Drawing: encourage children to think in images. For example, can they think about the house of the three bears and describe the garden?
- Draw alongside the child, making your thinking explicit: for example, 'Now, I'm drawing the dinosaur's tail – it's very long and gets thinner and thinner'.
- Drawing and writing: observe children's drawings carefully and point out any examples of early letter formation. For example, 'I think that is a letter in your name, Aaron'.
- Share many books which have simple captions to supplement the illustrations: leave these around as models for mark-making.

Support early mathematical thinking

- Mathematical graphics: encourage children to use tallies. For example, to use clip boards to identify the number of people who have brought welly boots to go outside, who have brought a packed lunch, etc.
- Counting skills: recognise their interest in personal numbers. For example, who has the most letters in their name? Who has the fewest letters?
- Practise numbers for counting: introduce number rhymes and encourage children to practise these when playing with number rhyme boxes (containing small-scale figures). For example, 5 little ducks, 10 children in a bed.
- Thinking about shape, space and measures: display and refer to images showing the sequence of the day, encourage children to measure and mark their partner's height using a height chart.

Case Study 5.4

Predicting and checking

A reception teacher prepared attractively wrapped parcels, bulky items that were light in weight, those that were heavy, small heavy items and those that were light. She invited a child to select a parcel and predict if it was heavy or light. She then threw the chosen parcel to the child who checked out his prediction. After children had become familiar with the game, they were encouraged to play it for themselves and later to wrap up their own surprise parcels.

Comment

The enjoyable game helped children to understand that size does not always equate with weight. The teacher modelled the game and then handed responsibility over to the children to play in their own way.

- Spaces and locations: help children to consider spaces and locations when building dens; display many examples of maps and plans, for example, architects' plans in the block area; encourage children to draw a map to show teddy how to find their house; plan a simple trip to the shops and, together, discuss the route and draw a map.

Support thinking about the world

- Urge children to **observe in depth**: to look and listen, smell and taste, and handle things again, and each time to discuss with others what more they have found out; encourage a child to return to an initial record (drawing, model, photograph) of their first observation and consider if they need to add anything else.
- Encourage contact with natural materials: to help children understand their properties and how they **change**, for example, through pulling, pushing, freezing, heating, or when water is added; when change is permanent or when it can be reversed; to help them to predict what might happen and to base predictions on evidence from their past experiences (rather than just guessing).
- Foster **speculation and enquiry**: encourage children to put forward their own ideas about why things happen or how things work. For example, 'I think that plants die to make room for lots of other plants', 'My dad's motorbike works because he pumps petrol into the tyres'.

- Take children's scientific questions seriously, for example, 'why do my nails grow?', 'what made that big rock?'; open children's ideas and questions to the group and invite the views of others, contributing to a 'pool of thought'.

Promoting intentional thinking

In Chapter 4 we saw how intentional behaviour enables young children to regulate their actions and begin to take control of their thinking. In this chapter we look at the following ways to support children in becoming intentional thinkers:

- by providing a climate which supports development of self-regulation
- by promoting a management style which allows children scope to think
- by developing a thinking-friendly environment
- by encouraging self-regulated thinking and metacognition.

A climate which supports the development of self-regulation

Self-regulation involves helping young children to manage their behaviour, feelings and social contacts with others as well as their thoughts and ideas. Consequently, a supportive climate must link to these aspects.

The following conditions help children's thoughts to take root and flourish:

- when they are with adults they trust. If children feel comfortable in a setting and are familiar with the pattern of the day, they have the confidence and emotional vigour to develop their own ideas
- when they are encouraged to share their thoughts with others, both in self-chosen play and in small, informal discussion groups
- when they are given props to help structure and regulate their thoughts. Provide an attractive pictorial chart with the following headings: What do I want to do? Who do I want to do it with? What do I need in order to do it? How well did we do it?
- when they are free to make mistakes and encouraged to see these as a valuable way of learning. Occasionally, ask children if they have made a useful mistake during the day and what did they learn from it
- when they have time to pause and think, revisit and reconsider their thoughts, make connections and practise and apply what they know. Having become really familiar with materials, children are then able to use this knowledge to combine materials and develop more elaborate representations.

Practical Activity

Creating more time for children to think?

Aim to reduce the times when children are waiting for things to happen, for example, waiting for everyone to be ready to go into the hall or go outside, getting dressed after PE, clearing up at the end of the session, sitting down for a group snack, waiting for their turn to respond to the register.

Reduce registration times, for example, trust children to self-register and have a head count to check daily numbers.

Provide a self-service snack time.

Encourage children to use waiting times for thinking, for example, share a picture book with their thinking partner and question each other about what is happening in the pictures, plan for their play for the next session, listen to a piece of recorded music and think about the images it suggests.

A management style which supports intentional thinking

The way in which the daily programme operates can enable or restrict children's scope to think for themselves. Drawing on studies and my own observations, there seem to be broadly three management approaches (23, 24):

- A controlling or *programmed approach* is highly structured by the adult who makes all the decisions: for example, she decides on the resources that children use, the groups they work in, the location and time allocated to activities. Children feel safe and secure and respond to clear boundaries but the emphasis is on compliance. There is very little scope for initiative.
- An *open-framework approach* gives children good scope to make decisions in areas of learning, but the adult is visible to guide, support and monitor children's choices and explorations. The approach offers freedom but within adult boundaries.
- An *informational* or *child-centred approach* is based entirely on supporting children's interests. Children are encouraged to take responsibility for themselves by learning to plan their work, decide who to work with, what resources they need. The emphasis is on encouraging independence and creativity.

Most practitioners will adopt a mix of management styles to suit the purpose intended. The informational approach is most likely to give scope for young children's intentional thinking and action, and the

open-framework approach gives the practitioner a clear role in supporting these processes.

> ### Professional checkpoints
>
> Which management approach best describes my way of working with
> young children?
> What changes do I need to make to encourage children to think more for
> themselves?

A thinking-friendly environment

Young children have great scope to regulate their behaviour and thinking when engaged in their self-selected play. We have already suggested
how, by fostering young children's positive mind-sets, their social
encounters and emotional security, we strengthen their will and confidence to think and share their thoughts. Here we outline useful ways to
promote intentional thinking through the physical environment.

Continuous provision

The quality of resources and materials that are available on a daily basis
for young children has an important impact on the quality of their
thinking. If a child plans to construct a castle but only has one set of
plastic bricks, his bold and imaginative intentions come to a halt. If he
only has one type of adhesive to fix materials together, he is unable to
make informed decisions about what is fit for his purpose. A rich range
of continuous provision will allow young children to work in a familiar
environment where they can select and use materials, extend their skills,
represent their thoughts and ideas in different ways, and link some ideas
together.

Enhancing continuous provision

Providing enhancements to basic continuous provision allows children's
individual interests to be catered for, for example, making connections
with their home interests.

Early Excellence, a principled and exemplary training and resource
centre, suggests that continuous provision indoors can be enhanced by:

- New books – to support a particular interest, season or festival
- Images and resources – to develop an interactive display around a
  particular idea of interest

- Resource collections – to enrich a provision such as sand in miniature
- Focused collections – to explore a particular concept, such as colour or light.

Enhancements to continuous provision outdoors include:

- Role-play resources – to extend events such as camping, BBQ, picnics
- Investigative resources – such as exploring windy weather, bubbles
- Resource collections – to introduce and develop maths games, pattern-making and mark-making
- Horticultural collections – to add stimulus to growing and gardening (25).

Making provision accessible

A well-ordered layout for continuous provision means that children know where each piece of apparatus is stored and can retrieve it easily. Attention to detail when organising equipment should make it possible for children to use the environment as a workshop.

- Ensure that children are familiarised with all areas of learning; introduce new children to each area in turn and show them the possibilities for exploration and enquiry; suggest that experienced players to help less experienced children
- Encourage children to remind one another where resources are located
- Where children return to one provision again and again, remind them of the range of alternative options that are available
- Create a space for everything and avoid over-crowding equipment
- Check that all equipment is visible, stored at the child's level and that lids on containers fit properly.

Professional checkpoint

Reflect how well your displayed environment supports children's thoughts and ideas.

Using the displayed environment

- **Make children's thinking visible.** Display their thoughts on a prominent 'What we think?' board. This immediately raises the status of thinking. As a thinking companion, contribute your thoughts: 'Danny thought..., Mrs Dowling thought...'.

- **Display the processes of work**. Displays of children's work in various stages of completion will help them to remember and refer to what they have done already and how they might take it further.
- **Keep displays fresh and alive**. Support young children's visual memory by asking them to look out for change in one area of the room. When children enter the setting the following day you may have turned a picture upside down, removed or substituted a different one. Make the memory game more complex over time and involve children in making the changes.
- **Provide interactive displays**. Children become more involved in displays that they can touch, use or to which they can contribute: display images of faces with different expressions that they can discuss; provide a storyboard with images of characters and buildings that they can move around to create different scenarios; bring in a working machine/vehicle, such as a bicycle, that they can explore and investigate to see how it works.
- **Encouraging social play**. Building dens offers wonderful scope for children to collaborate (you can't build a den by yourself), exchange ideas, argue, negotiate and learn to compromise.

Professional checkpoint

Does your provision for den making:
- give priority to children's thoughts and ideas?
- allow children an illusion of privacy?
- make children aware of the rich range of continuous provision that is available to them, for example:

   o outside: bushes, trees, tree trunks, logs, pieces of wood, tarpaulins, old curtains, rugs, mats, broom handles, wooden clothes horse, windbreaks, car and tractor tyres?
   o inside/outside: milk crates, large cardboard and wooden boxes, fabrics, masking tape, wooden pegs, tent pegs, rope, string, garden ties, bulldog clips, old cupboard without doors, pillows, blankets?

- include images of different dens and suggestions for what resources they might want to use?
- offer guidance and technical advice if children need it?
- include records:

   o take photographs of the various stages of building and encourage children to do so?
   o display the photographs alongside examples of families camping/ animal dens?
   o involve sharing the images with children and encouraging them to recall and compare their experiences?

Case Study 5.5

Dieter, a quiet four year old, had been in the nursery for just one month. He tended to wander and watch other children without joining in their play. In conversation with Dieter's dad, Rose, Dieter's key person, learned that Dieter had become interested in lighthouses having seen one during a family outing to the coast. The next day Rose read the story of *The Lighthouse Keeper's Lunch* to her key group. Later, she noted that Dieter was poring over the book, which she had left in the book area. Rose joined him, seeming to be engaged in another book. Dieter brought his book to her and pointed to the lighthouse.

> *Dieter*: 'I've seen one like that.'
> *Rose*: 'Well, I expect you know a lot about lighthouses then, don't you Dieter?'
> *Dieter*: 'I could make one.'
> *Rose*: 'Go on then – there are lots of things you could use in the making area.'
> *Dieter*: 'I'll make one that lights up – lighthouses do that to warn the boats… to stop them drowning.'

Dieter spent two sessions working continuously, often muttering to himself about what he was going to do next. In response to his request, Rose helped him create a circuit to light his construction. Other children were intrigued by the lighthouse and Dieter proudly told them about its function and showed them how it worked. He also told them about the lighthouse keeper who lived there with one seagull friend who was magic and caught fish for their dinner.

Comment

By providing a relevant story, Rose helped Dieter to recall his memory of the lighthouse and encouraged him to represent the memory through his construction. His 'private talk' helped to regulate his actions. The rich range of recycled and natural materials available allowed Dieter to select and discard and eventually decide on the most appropriate 'stuff' to best re-create his lighthouse. He had as much time and adult support as he needed to work in depth and achieve completion to his satisfaction. Dieter extended this thinking by developing an imaginative story using narrative language.

Encourage self-regulated thinking and metacognition

Having established a climate, management style and environment that help children to regulate their thinking, this final section highlights a few important ways for practitioners to further support young children's intentions.

Progress choosing to planning

Vygotsky believed that planning play was a powerful way to expand learning and this approach is being used in an American programme *Tools of the Mind*. The children involved are helped to think ahead and act based on those thoughts (26).

Young children's choices in play can become more deliberate and focused if:

- they are encouraged to consider and plan their intentions on a daily basis. It is important that at this stage the key person works informally with children individually or in small groups; each child needs the practitioner's full attention and the opportunity to put their plan into action as soon as possible rather than spend time listening to other children; young children may elect to give a brief verbal plan or provide an image (drawing, photograph) indicating what they have in mind
- they are aware of what materials are available inside and outside to support their intentions
- practitioners help them to elaborate their plans through companionable enquiries sensitively dropped at times into conversations: 'So where will you build this big fire engine?', 'Who is going to work with you?', 'What will you need?', 'What will you do first?'

Progress recall to reflection

Young children's recall or memory of their experiences can become more evaluative if:

- they have plenty of time to contemplate the effects of their actions; ask one or two children only in a review session to reflect and report on their work; chair the session and encourage other children to ask questions
- they start to think about what went well and what they might have learned from any mistakes
- they are encouraged to think back to their original intention and ponder whether it was achieved
- the practitioner scribes and displays some reflections using the exact words that children use.

Support sustained endeavours which are the context for sustained thinking

As children reflect on their experiences, they may recall problems they encountered or spin-offs they have not anticipated. These observations create a perfect opportunity for them to try different solutions or build on newly discovered interests the following day. (27)

So young children's sustained endeavours can be supported if:

- they are encouraged to place a 'please leave' sign by an unfinished piece of work
- limited space prevents children leaving their work, they might take a photograph of a partially finished project; this will act as a reminder of the stage that they reached in the first draft of their work and provide a link to what they will do this time to improve it further.

Use encouragement rather than praise

Pam Lafferty, the director of High Scope UK, usefully distinguishes between 'praise' and 'encouragement'. Lafferty suggest that praise comes from 'outside the child and is an external judgement of approval', while 'encouragement' is about motivating the child within and creating the ongoing desire to learn (28). Children can become dependent on praise, which can become a form of regulation. However, encouragement, particularly if it is specific rather than general, helps self-regulation by affirming an action and helping children to reflect on their competencies.

Help young children to think about their thinking

Metacognition is thinking about one's thinking and consciously using different thinking strategies to solve problems. This is considered further in Chapters 6 and 7. Before five years, children's metacognitive abilities are just emerging. However, Fisher suggests that this form of higher level thinking may be related to experience rather than age, and that practitioners can help young children become more aware of their thinking tools and how they can use them (29). Donaldson summarises: 'If the child is going to control and direct his own thinking, in the way we have been considering, [self-regulation] he must become conscious of it' (30).

Practitioners can support metacognition by:

- playing games which introduce specific thinking skills. For example, Kim's Game (memory skills), reading stories and inviting prediction, showing an intriguing object, such as a conch shell, and asking 'what can it be?' (enquiry skills).
- being explicit about your own thinking processes. Young children need to recognise how much thinking you use in your work – remembering to take the register, planning the play resources to put out each day, questioning children about their play intentions, enquiring about the arrangements for a local outing.
- helping children to become aware of the thinking processes that they will need for a task. For example, 'Now when making up our own story of the gingerbread man, we must try to remember the story in the book, we must share our thoughts for some new adventures for

the gingerbread man, and we must agree about an exciting ending for the story'.
- infusing the language of thinking on a daily basis. Children will start to be more aware of the different ways in which they think if the terms are used regularly (see Professional checkpoint below).
- ensuring that children are interested. Although it appears that early awareness of thinking is present from a young age, once again, studies suggest that children will only bother to learn to use and develop thinking strategies if they are convinced that it is worthwhile (31).

Professional checkpoint

Help children to become aware of different ways of thinking that they can use:

- Easy thinking (memorising)
- Hard thinking (making connections)
- Think about a picture in your head (visualising)
- Think about what comes first, next... (sequencing)
- Think about what happened yesterday (recalling)
- Think about what might happen (predicting)
- Think about finding out (enquiring)
- Think about what you know already (early schema)
- Think how well you have done (reflecting/evaluating)

Key points for working with parents

Help parents to recognise the importance of their child's friendships and the value of inviting friends home.
Share information about the transition to reception; ask parents to tell you of any anxieties that their child has about the forthcoming move.
Suggest to parents that they encourage their child to:

- make plans about what they do with their time at home – play inside or outside, draw, dress up
- at the end of the day, remember and think about what they have done – what they have most enjoyed and why.

Useful books

Bright, P. and Wildish, L. (2009) *Charlie's Superhero Underpants*. London: Little Tiger Press.
Wonderfully humorous and engaging about brave Charlie's journey to retrieve his lost underpants. A good antidote to violent super-hero stories.

Browne, A. (1999) *Voices in the Park*. London: Random House.
Exploring different perspectives of people, with some surreal images.

Deacon, A. (2004) *Beegu*. London: Red Fox.
A thought-provoking story about the experiences of a little creature who arrives on earth and is lost.

Hughes, S. (2004) *Don't Want To Go*. London: Red Fox.
A reassuring tale about trying new things.

References

1. Brierley, J. (1994) *Give Me a Child until He is Seven* (2nd edn). Lewes: Falmer Press.
2. Cousins, J. (1990) 'Are Your Little Humpty Dumpties Floating or Sinking? What Sense Do Children of Four Make of the Reception Class at School?', *Early Years*, 10(2), Spring: 28–38.
3. Department for Children, Schools and Families (DCFS) (2008) *The National Strategies: Early Years Social and Emotional Aspects of Development (SEAD).* Guidance for Practitioners in the EYFS. London: DCFS, p. 50.
4. Qualifications and Curriculum Development Agency (QDCA) (2008) *EYFSP Handbook*. Available at: www.qcda.gov.uk (order online: code QCA/08/3657/), p. 4.
5. DCFS (2008) *The National Strategies* (see note 3).
6. Dunn, J. (2004) *Children's Friendships*. Oxford: Blackwell, p. 31.
7. Smith, P.K., Cowie, H. and Blades, M. (2003) *Understanding Children's Development* (2nd edn). Oxford: Blackwell.
8. McTavish, A. (2007) *Feelings and Behaviour: A Creative Approach*. London: Early Education, p. 10.
9. Siren Films (1990) *Falling Out*. Newcastle: Siren Film and Video Ltd.
10. Broadhead, P. (2004) *Early Years Play and Learning*. Oxford: Routledge.
11. Wainryb, L., Shaw, A., Langley, M., Cotton, K. and Lewis, R. (2004) 'Children's Thinking about Diversity of Belief in the Early School Years: Judgements of Relatism, Tolerance and Disagreeing Persons', *Society for Research in Child Development*, 75(3): 687–703.
12. Robson, S. (2006) *Developing Thinking and Understanding in Young Children*. Oxford: Routledge, p. 48.
13. Athey, C. (2007) *Extending Thought in Young Children: A Parent–Teacher Partnership* (2nd edn). London: Sage.
14. Department for Education and Skills (DfES) (2007) *Principles into Practice Cards: 3.4 The Wider Context, 3.2 Supporting Every Child*. London: DfES.
15. Read, V. (2010) *Developing Attachment in Early Years Settings*. London: Routledge, p. 73.
16. Edwards, C., Gandini, L. and Forman, G. (1993) *The Hundred Languages of Children: The Reggio Emilia Approach to Early Childhood Education*. Norwood, NJ: Ablex, p. 78.
17. Drummond, M.J. (1993) *Assessing Children's Learning*. London: David Fulton, p. 59.

18. Craft, A., (2010) in 'Creative Thinking and Creative Development', quoted in Department for Children, Schools and Families, *Finding and Exploring Young Children's Fascinations: National Strategies Early Years*. London: DCFS, p. 13.
19. Sure Start, Department for Education and Skills/Primary National Strategy (2005) *Communicating Matters*. Module 1: Day 2, Focus 5. London: DfES, pp. 64–8.
20. Ibid., Module 2: Day 1, Focus 4, pp. 37–45.
21. Department for Children, Schools and Families (DCFS) (2008) *Every Child a Talker: Guidance for Early Language Lead Practitioner*. London: DCFS.
22. Bromley, H. (2011) *Come Alive Superheroes Resources Pack*. Cambridge: Yellow Door. Available at: www.yellow-door.net.
23. Deci, E.L. and Ryan, R.M. (1985) *Intrinsic Motivation and Self-determination*. New York: Plenum Press.
24. Siraj-Blatchford, I. (2008) 'Understanding the Relationship between Curriculum Pedagogy and Progression in Learning in Early Childhood', *Hong Kong Journal of Early Childhood*, 7(2): 10–12.
25. Marsden, L. and Woodbridge, J. (2005) *Looking Closely at Learning and Teaching: A Journey of Development*. Huddersfield: Early Excellence Ltd (available at: www.earlyexcellence.com), p. 8.
26. Bodrova, E. and Leong, D.J. (2004) *Tools of the Mind*. Boston, Massachusetts: Allyn and Bacon.
27. Epstein, A.S. (2003) 'How Planning and Reflection Develop Young Children's Thinking Skills', *Beyond the Journal: Young Children on the Web*, September. Washington: National Association for the Education of Young Children.
28. Lafferty, P. (2008) 'Child-initiated Learning – A View from High Scope', in S. Featherstone and P. Featherstone (eds), *Like Bees Not Butterflies*. London: A & C Black.
29. Fisher, R. (1998) 'Thinking about Thinking: Developing Metacognition in Children', *Early Child Development and Care*, 141: 1–15.
30. Donaldson, M. (1978) *Children's Minds*. London: Fontana, p. 94.
31. Meadows, S. and Cashdan, A. (1988) *Helping Children Learn*. London: David Fulton.

Brimming with Thoughts at Home and in School: Children's Thinking 5–7 Years

Intentions

This chapter:

- recognises how:
  - children build on their early experiences when developing their thinking during the early school years
  - children's thoughts and ideas are most powerful when they are involved in what interests them and are with friends
- understands how children:
  - draw on and deepen their schema and elaborate their play as they secure concepts
  - move into more abstract thinking and abstract representations
  - use their extended communication skills to support and sustain their thinking
  - increasingly control and apply their thinking intentionally through self-regulation

A shift in development

In this chapter we consider children's development and thinking as they move from the Early Years Foundation Stage into Years 1 and 2. Although five year olds in a reception class were included in the last chapter, we recognise that many of these young children are already in Year 1 and their needs must be considered in this context.

(Ages of transfer differ: in Wales they remain in the Foundation Stage until seven years of age; in Scotland they move into Primary 1 and 2 at six and seven years; in Northern Ireland children are in the Foundation Stage between four and six years, and Key Stage 1 ages 6–8 years.)

In the years between five and seven there is a recognised 'shift in development', but this appears to be most detectable around age seven years. As Julie Fisher points out, there is little evidence to show that the developmental characteristics of six year olds are any different from those of five year olds. Indeed, the more recent literature on child development refers to five to seven year olds and sometimes five to eight years as one phase (1, 2). Fisher also makes the important point that despite there being no notable differences between children learning at five and six, the range of development within one age group can vary considerably (3). This of course applies to all age groups described in this book.

So far we have described the ways in which young minds unfold during the first five years. In the best circumstances, they will have had a rich range of experiences to feed and provoke their thinking, with close adults in schools and at home acting as thinking companions. This provides the bedrock for the next phase in their thinking.

Information about how children think during the early primary years is thin when compared to the abundant research and evidence about child development in early years. However, it's helpful to look at two studies that give us some insights into the capabilities and characteristics of these older children.

Findings from an American paediatric study suggest that children from around 6–8 years:

- are more independent from their family
- have a stronger sense of right and wrong
- are becoming more aware of the future
- have a growing understanding about their place in the world
- focus more on teamwork and friendships
- are keen to become accepted and liked by friends
- become less focused on themselves and more concerned about others
- develop mental skills rapidly
- are more able to describe experiences and talk about thoughts and feelings (4).

An NFER research project showed that, by the age of seven most children are competent thinkers who are able to:

- use thinking language involving words such as 'think', 'know', 'guess' and 'remember'
- construct informal rules for the purpose of solving problems
- sort objects according to one or more criteria
- understand that the beliefs of others may be different from their own

- understand that because someone has partial knowledge of something they will not necessarily have all of it
- hypothesise about what might happen to future events
- suggest alternative actions that could have been taken in the past
- reason logically from given precepts (5).

These are tremendous achievements within the first seven years of life and need to be acknowledged. But the NFER list of thinking competencies is limited and arid when compared with what practitioners know, namely that children are capable of much more, for example, in developing imaginative, resourceful and innovative ideas. However, as we have seen, competent and sparkly thinking is dependent on the right conditions being available. In this chapter we see how six and seven year olds develop additional skills and aptitudes to think, but the will to use their minds remains the imperative.

Maintaining a disposition to think

Finding the Element

Claxton suggests that a skill is something that we *can* do whereas a disposition is something that we *do* (6). Children moving into the primary years will already have acquired many skills to think but they need to be motivated to use them. A series of German studies looked at changes in children's motivation linked to their age and cognitive development (7). Findings indicate that before the age of 11 years, children do not see a clear distinction between effort and ability. If their friend achieves a complex drawing or produces some early writing, they are not aware that this may be because the child spent considerable time and endeavour on achieving it or simply found it easy. This implies that six and seven year olds do not explicitly recognise the benefits of persevering and making an effort. They will only use these traits if they are inclined or minded to do so. As we saw in Chapter 4, 'the passion for stretching yourself and sticking to it, even (or especially) when it's not going well, is the hallmark of the growth mind-set' (8).

So where do children find this passion? Ken Robinson suggests that it is when they are in their 'Element'. He describes the features for being in the 'Element' as the meeting point between natural aptitude and personal passion, and the conditions for being in it are attitude and opportunity. He says that when people are in their Element:

> they are doing the thing they love, and in doing it they feel like their most authentic selves. ... They connect to something fundamental to their sense of identity, purpose and well-being. (9)

Surely there are some messages here for children who have moved away from infancy and who are on the edge of new horizons for thinking. Let's explore the features and conditions described above in relation to children aged 5–7 years.

Aptitude is having an ability or capability to do something. In the best circumstances during the first five years of life, children will have had many and various opportunities to explore and experiment freely; they will also have had time to rehearse and repeat experiences as they incubate and hatch new thoughts and ideas. During these rich years children will have learned new skills and concepts and become curious about certain phenomena. Later in this chapter we see how their early schema are the precursors to later concepts and how they extend what they know through further developing their language skills.

Children can be proficient at doing something without it involving their feelings. Passion involves emotions. Being in the Element means having a profound satisfaction and joy in what one is doing. Having had wide opportunities to select experiences that interest them, children stand a good chance of finding something that absorbs them. This deep interest is not likely to be permanent, but while it lasts the child is working at a deep level of involvement and experiencing high well-being, as described in Chapter 4.

Attitude is closely aligned to mind-set, described in the previous chapter. Children with positive mind-sets relish the challenges, different experiences and ways of thinking that are involved as they move into a new class. Others who have a fixed mind-set may have been comfortable in the reception class but fear possible changes and challenges ahead, which they do not feel equipped to deal with.

Around seven years children are becoming more aware of themselves in relation to others in their class. They have sharpened insights into their abilities, become self-critical about what they can achieve and are sensitive to the comments of others (10). Their intentions are not always fulfilled if they do not have the technical expertise and skills to create what they have in mind. This can cause frustration and all children experience vexation at times. However, the way in which it is dealt with is the important distinguishing factor. Those with positive mind-sets will grapple with difficulty, persevere and be optimistic. The fixed mind-set children cannot face a hitch in their thinking and learning and are in danger of giving up.

Creative and critical thinking, as we have seen, involves making connections. Such higher level thinking is hard work for children; they need to be energised and positively disposed to think and link their ideas together. This energy, commitment and tenacity can lead children to experience huge satisfactions reaped from their endeavours, even if they don't recognise the reasons for their achievements.

Ken Robinson points out that our aptitudes will only be realised if the opportunities are there, the implication being that lack of prospect can prevent people from achieving their Element. Adults are able to create opportunities by seeking out kindred spirits, planning new adventures or changing jobs. Children cannot always make these choices; they may have the potential to be deep and creative thinkers, but not have the opportunity to release their talents. The ways in which we can create opportunities for five, six and seven year olds to apply their minds are discussed in the next chapter.

Social understandings: thinking with friends and as one of a group

Why do friendships matter?

Studies indicate that the best predictor of adapting to adult life is not to do with cognitive achievements but rather with the success with which children get along with other children. Those who are unable to sustain close relationships with their peers are seen to be extremely disadvantaged (11). This strong statement is based on several reasons:

- **Friendships support transitions**. Bearing in mind how a transition can affect children's thinking both positively and negatively, friends can play an important role. This emerged as a major theme in Judy Dunn's research. She asked children who had been in school for six weeks what advice they would give to a child who was about to start. One boy gave a clear message – 'get a friend' (12). The friendships that children made in the nursery serve them in good stead when they start school. Dunn goes further and suggests that the quality of relationships that they have with friends when they start school can influence the way in which children at five and six years cope with the demands of a new school (13).
- **Social intelligence**. Friends come to matter more and more during the early school years and children become very aware of the complexities of relationships during the school day. For example, they know who plays with who during playtimes and their preferences for seating in the classroom. They now identify with a group away from the family and develop a loyalty to a group of friends they play with and an affiliation to their class.
- **Moral understandings**. Helwig and Turiel explained that Piaget viewed moral development as moving from adherence to right and wrong when directed by adults, to behaving morally from their own motives 'in which rules are understood as social constructions

formulated in social relations of co-operation with peers' (14). Notions of fairness and justice become important and children understand the need to take turns and heed the rules of a game. The more mature children think and behave considerately from the pull of their conscience rather than because it is required of them from adults.

- **Thinking about others' minds.** Once a friendship begins to develop, the opportunities for the children involved to learn about what this other person feels and thinks increases markedly (15). In order for children to sustain a friendship they must develop skills of empathy and become sensitive to others' minds. In Chapter 4 we see that 3–4 years olds are already learning about how to maintain friendships. These insights are strengthened in school relationships. Although older children still argue and jealousies and confrontations are just as common, by contrast, at 6–7 years children are more able to understand their friends' perpectives. This is marked by less self-absorption and increased care and concern for others. Once again, the seeds are sown during the early years. Judy Dunn's study indicates that where children at three years had been able to understand the thoughts, feeling and beliefs of others, this continued in school life and was evidenced by long conversations, elaborate play and recognition of others' views (16). This increased knowledge and understanding that older children build in friendships means that they are able to resolve altercations more skilfully using conciliation, compromise and reasoning skills in order to come to an agreement and maintain the relationship. Moreover, Dunn's study shows that these social understanding and use of sophisticated skills were most evident in the context of friendship rather than with other social contacts or within the family (17).
- **Support for cognitive development.** When working by themselves children can achieve so much, but when working with others their thinking and learning expands. Vygotsky's views on the value of children's social thinking are supported by Azmitia's study. She observed five year olds working in pairs and came up with the following conclusions:

  o Having a partner can increase the amount of time children work on a task.
  o The presence of a partner can help a child persevere on a task and it can add enjoyment to the activity.
  o When children work together they often increase their total work strategies as different children bring different strategies to an activity.
  o When less experienced or less mature children are paired with an older or more able partner, the 'novice' learns a great deal from observing her 'expert' partner (18).

Another study showed that peer support can include: **peer tutoring**, where a more informed child offers information to one less experienced; **co-operative learning**, where children combine to solve problems and develop new ideas; **peer collaboration**, where children work together on something that neither can do alone; **peer modelling**, where one child learns from another's demonstration. Once again, this study shows that these forms of support are more prominent and effective between friends – yet another indication of the link between these intimate relations, frequent conversations and mutual understandings that exist in friendships (19).

Case Study 6.1

Having seen a TV programme on a team of explorers making a base camp, Kieran was very keen to build a camp in a wild area in the school grounds. Children in Years 1 and 2 had free access to this area during lunch times. Kieran told his friends Ali and Isaac of his intentions and said that they could watch him. He selected a low branched tree as the location for this camp and collected together some materials seemingly at random, including two large cardboard boxes, some drapes and ropes. At this point Kieran seemed to run out of steam.

> *Ali*:   'So what will you do now?'
> *Kieran*: 'Shut up, I know what to do.'
> *Ali*:   [not deterred] 'You need a roof don't you.'

[No response from Kieran who looks dejected and at a loss]

> *Ali*:   [trying another approach] 'That looks great Kieran. I think that you are really ace at building camps.'
> *Isaac*:   'Yeah, I think it's good.'
> *Ali*:   'It will look really, really good when you put the roof on and when you make some stuff with those boxes.'
> *Kieran*: 'If you help me I'm still the boss.'
> *Ali*:   'I know, you tell people what to do, don't you?'

Comment

Ali was extremely skilled at reading Kieran's mind. He quickly realised that Kieran could not progress in his camp building. When his advice about adding a roof fell on stony ground he tried praise and appeasement. Kieran gratefully accepted this conciliatory approach and was mollified. In turn he suggested a compromise to allow his friend to work with him. Ali agreed to co-operate and the relationship remained intact.

Making sense

Development of schemas leading to later concepts

We have seen how babies and infants use actions and sensory experiences to develop schema and come to know about things. At three and four years they think about schema in more abstract ways, through talk and mark-making, and their schema often form the basis of understanding about different concepts.

As schema are strengthened and patterns of thinking are secured, they become stored in children's implicit or hidden memories. When close adults refer to, support and enrich these stored schema with content, they help the child to recall and consolidate what he has learned already.

Case Study 6.2

Six year old Sara was engrossed watching dragonflies zooming around a pond.

Mum: 'Do you remember, Sara, when you were very little dad made you a paper aeroplane and you used to whizz it round the garden. And you always wanted me to read you that book about fairies. I bought you some fairy wings and you pretended that you could fly.'

Sara: 'Oh yes, yes, I loved those wings and I always drew fairies. But I could never fly as well as those dragonflies. But people are more heavy, aren't they, so it would be difficult.'

Comment

When mum encouraged Sara to recall her early interests in flying, she helped her to bring implicit memories (stored schema) alive and consolidate them. Sara now starts to think about how weight can affect flight.

Each scheme of thought is concerned with a fragment or aspect of information. In Chapter 4 we saw how children develop and combine their schema; by so doing they consolidate their understandings and form early concepts in order to generalise about what they know. With additional experience they assimilate more complex ideas which are the forerunners to concepts in subjects of the National Curriculum (see box below).

Some early schema linked to concepts in subjects of the National Curriculum

Early Schema	Later Concepts
Vertical trajectory	Height – maths, time lines – history
Horizontal trajectory	Flight – science, angles – maths
Lateral trajectory	Graphs co-ordinates – maths – joinery – design
Grid	Charts – history, maths, structures – design
Trajectory	Shading, scribbling – art
	Moving and handling – physical
Dab	Aiming at a point, using a compass, for example radius of a circle on a circumference – maths
Enclosing	Shapes – maths, figure drawing – art
Containing and enveloping	Surrounding and covering an area – art, capacity and volume – maths
Transporting	Quantity and understanding of numbers – maths

In Chapter 2 we noted that children's schema operate at four different levels, namely, sensorimotor, symbolic, functional dependency and abstract thought. Chris Athey suggests that:

> When children reach the 'thought level', the earlier motor and representational stages, with all the contents of past experience, are 'brought forward' to provide the 'form' and 'stuff' of thinking. As with all schemas, paucity or richness of experience becomes increasingly apparent with age. (20)

In order for a child to properly understand a concept (shown in the above box) Nuttall believes that he needs to demonstrate his co-ordinated set of schema in different ways at least three times (21).

Case Study 6.3

Two year old Dana was absorbed putting things in containers, placing a lid on the container, tipping things out and starting again.

At two years ten months she painted a picture, telling her key person that 'This is me in bed.' She then returned to the picture and covered it in paint. 'I cover me up.'

(Continued)

(Continued)

When helping to clear up, Dana (now three years) said that she needed a bigger box for the small bricks. 'They keep falling out, there isn't enough room. Bricks need more room to fit in.'

In Year 1 Dana and her friend loved building homes. They co-operated in making a roof for their home using a blanket and wooden props. 'We must make sure that there are no holes', said Dana, 'or water will get into our house.' The girls then considered how they could divide the space in their den. 'We have to fit in a bed and a chair in this space', said Dana.

Having allocated the space and furnished it with a sleeping bag and chair, the children took photographs of 'their home' to share with their families.

Comment

Dana's early enveloping schema is observed through her actions (motor level), through her drawing (symbolic level), through recognising capacity by filling a box with bricks (functional dependency). These experiences culminate in her understanding of 'covering' an area and sub-dividing a space. Dana's schema, demonstrated at different levels helped her concept development. She also strengthened her thinking by working in a pleasurable context – sharing with a friend and engaged in doing something that she enjoyed. By sharing the photos and describing how they made the construction, both girls recalled the processes of their thinking.

Pretend and fantasy play

Julie Fisher is unequivocal in the need for children in school to continue to play:

> At this age, play remains a driving force for children discovering about themselves and the world around them. However sophisticated young children may seem in many situations, given open spaces the most basic of resources they love to involve themselves in fantasy, 'super hero', imaginative, exploratory play. (22)

Her views are supported by our daily observations of children at play where they remain absorbed for long periods and appear to be in the Element. Although at six and seven years children are taught thinking skills (see Chapter 7), play is a vehicle for practising and applying these skills. Paley describes play as the glue that binds together the early teaching of reading and writing skills (23). These words echo Vygotsky's message that writing should be cultivated rather than imposed and that in play children find purposes to read and write together (24).

Because there are no restrictions set in developing children's ideas and thoughts in play, they can imagine to the limits of their capabilities. Fisher's Oxfordshire research shows many examples of more able children engaging in high-level learning through play (25).

Continued development of children's fantasy play linked to popular culture

Children's play is enriched by increased experiences and interests, including continuing exposure to popular culture (Case Study 6.4). At 6–7 years, many children's worlds are informed by TV, DVD, films, computer games and comics. At this age, they have conscious control over their imagination and will select the content that holds their interest. Children find aspects of popular culture compelling and invest their energies in exploring related issues. By now they are able to bring in new scenarios to the play and consider different consequences from the ones they have experienced in film and print. Moreover, because they are now more able to consider other points of view and play co-operatively, their play becomes more elaborated and reciprocal.

Children's appetite for different media texts is shown in their mark-making and writing. Graham's small-scale study investigating use of popular culture in writing found that children in reception and Year 2 classes chose to represent these worlds in their writing journals (adults scribed for the younger children). In both year groups, boys made a substantial number of entries, which included exploring their appetite for football and comic characters. The boys chatted freely, sharing their creations and making meaning together. The author concluded that the children's work flourished as they showed what they could do given the opportunity to bring their home interests into the classroom and present these worlds in their chosen ways, using design, illustrations and words (26).

Case Study 6.4

During a visit to a reception class I chatted to five year old Isabel about her views of school life. She appeared only moderately enthusiastic about the daily programme but said that she most loved playtimes. I innocently asked her if she played skipping games outside and in return received a withering response.

'No of course not, we play "Casualty" and I'm Chloe (a central character).'

(Continued)

(Continued)

Isabel continued, showing real animation. 'Do you know, I love it, playing Chloe I mean. When I go to bed at night, I start to think about all the things that Chloe might do next day.'

Isabel's teacher, Maria, listened to the conversation, smiling.

Maria: 'So perhaps in class discussion time we could hear later what the Casualty staff have been up to Isabel.'

Comment

Maria described Isabel as a very sociable child with a vivid imagination but who found it difficult to listen and concentrate in most adult-led activities. She quickly realised that Isabel's energies and enthusiasm were most evident in fantasy play derived from viewing a popular TV series. Maria admitted that initially she had ignored this, but had recently shown an interest in the play and had encouraged the players to reflect on the play themes and consider alternative scenarios to the ones depicted in the programme. She found that the children were fluent in relating familiar content but also ingenious in their suggestions for further developments. Isabel and her friend had also started to draw some of the characters and write captions to describe their roles.

Routes into abstract thinking

We saw earlier in the book how babies and young children make meaning through movement, play and developing multi-modal images. These forms of representation continue to be important but now children are moving into more abstract thinking. By around seven years, children become more able to imagine and think about a problem without trying it out. They are not so dependent on hands-on experiences and are starting to move beyond the here and now.

Piaget, cited in Bruce, Meggitt and Grenier, suggests that seven year olds are starting to move into the stage of concrete operations, shown in their growing abilities to:

- hold in mind several things at once
- deepen the ways they use symbols as they write, read and use mathematical graphics/numbers
- conserve ideas about shape, number, quantities and volume (understand the need to see beyond how things look)
- understand the rules of games (27).

This greater freedom of abstract thought allows children to transfer what they have learned from one context to another. A child who has learned to sequence his thoughts (first, second, next) when telling a story is able to apply this sequencing skill when mixing paints and in mathematical pattern-making.

Children need to start to think in abstract ways in order to use formal symbol systems.

Inductive and deductive thinking

Children build their theories based on their experiences. They make sense through piecing these experiences together and applying one rule. This is inductive reasoning. Children will revise these thoughts only if they have further experiences which they mull over and discuss with others.

Case Study 6.5

Rachel read her group of six year olds two stories about wicked witches. In a recall session the following day the children had absorbed the messages in the story and, as a result, were convinced (induced) that all witches were wicked.

The following weekend at home, Duke viewed the DVD of *The Wizard of Oz* and was very impressed with the story. After talking about the story with his mum, he came to the conclusion that some witches are good. In school, he described the two witches and put forward his revised views to others in his group. The others would not be persuaded, having not experienced the DVD themselves.

Comment

In the light of additional experience, Duke has reconsidered and tempered his view that all witches are wicked. Other children will continue to hold on to their original beliefs until they encounter material which help them to amend (assimilate and accommodate new ideas) their thinking.

Older children use their additional experience to reason deductively by adopting a general principle which they apply to particular events. For example, they are familiar with basic mathematical and scientific principles, such as conservation of number, transformation and fair testing, and can use this knowledge to solve problems. However, six and seven year olds may also reason deductively if they are dealing with familiar ideas. This is evident where they use and apply their understandings about fairness and justice and the need for rules.

Some studies suggest that boys are better able to use deductive thinking at an earlier age than girls (28).

Moving into writing

In reception (often before) and the early primary years, children's use of symbols develops further into writing. Bodrova and Leong suggest that drawing is instrumental in helping children to achieve the complex skill of written speech (29), but we should note warnings from Anning and Ring that 'children should not be made to feel that drawing is only a "temporary" holding form of symbolic representation leading to mastery of the "higher level" ability to form letters and numbers' (30).

Helen Bromley points out that 'although putting print on paper is the visible act of writing, it is important to acknowledge the invisible processes that come before'. She also rightly states that writing and thought are inseparable. 'The internal dialogue we have with ourselves from the moment that consciousness begins all contribute to our future experiences as writers' (31). Although children's writing development involves both composition (invisible) and transaction (visible) aspects, we are more concerned here with the thinking processes involved in generating texts.

Nigel Hall makes some useful points between children learning to write and becoming authors. He suggests that where a child is required to focus on the final product of a text with attention given to neatness and transcription, their thinking is restricted and their writing is simply to practise presentation skills. The move to authorship involves the child in reflective thinking. 'Authors are people who make decisions and are sensitive to what goes on the paper and are sensitive to the contexts in which they write and to the audiences for whom they write' (32). These are intellectual pursuits and they involve children using reasoning skills.

It can take some time for children to move on to transcribing their thoughts in words. In the next chapter we will consider how they can be supported.

Thinking mathematically

A great deal of mathematical development has already taken place since birth, noticeably when children are in real, everyday situations, described by Donaldson as embedded contexts (33).

The roots of development lie in the enriched experiences that they have encountered during their early years. Further thinking about maths will occur when children confront new problems and relate them to those that they have already experienced. For example, a child who has had lots of opportunities when clearing up to arrange and fit blocks into a storage box will be well placed to plan how to fit furniture into a play area.

Haylock and Cockburn state that children will extend their maths ideas by making connections between actions and concrete items, written symbols, spoken language and images. Two other processes help children make sense of their mathematical encounters:

- the notion of equivalence (recognising what is the same about a number of objects)
- transformation (understanding what is different or what has changed) (34).

Making these connections ensures that children come to a secure understanding of mathematics – without the connections, learning is simply by rote, with no thinking processes involved. Most children in the early primary years still need to use physical activity, handle real things, draw and talk about mathematics in order to make sense of formal mathematical symbols.

Pound and Lee suggest that mathematical thinking has its roots in imagination. They quote Devlin:

> The key to being able to think mathematically is to push this ability to 'fake reality' one step further into a realm that is purely symbolic. ... Mathematicians learn how to live in and reason about a purely symbolic world. (35)

This again highlights the power of fantasy play as a context for mathematical thinking.

Spoken language is also very important, although Worthington and Carruthers state that learning to talk mathematically is like learning a foreign language (36). Lee, cited in Pound, expands on this point. She suggests that unless pupils know the way that language is used in mathematics, they may believe that they do not understand a certain concept, when what they can't do is express the idea in language. Conversely, being able to express their mathematical ideas clearly enables pupils to recognise that they understand and can use mathematical ideas. Teachers will extend their pupils' ability to learn mathematics by helping them to express their ideas using appropriate language and by recognising that they need to use this language in a way that is different from their everyday use (37).

Children use talk to share ideas, for example, about the use of space when moving furniture into a play area or when laying out resources in small scale play. These discussions, alongside practical activity, help to secure mathematical concepts.

Given the opportunity, children aged 5–7 years are able to recall what they had learned in maths. One study, using playback of videotape used in a mathematics lesson, found that 85% of children involved could explain their mathematical thinking. One boy, Lucas said that he had learned 'how long things were and how short they were ... by counting the blocks' (38).

Children's scientific ideas

Developing scientific thinking is a gradual process and, as in mathematical thinking, it will only evolve as a child processes real experiences and adds these to extend their current understanding. Harlen describes a case study when 5–7 year olds were asked what they thought plants need to help them grow. The children commonly mentioned only one factor, such as soil, sun or water, but rarely all three. Nor did they make any attempt to explain why these conditions were needed (39). Children's drawings are again very useful in communicating their ideas. When asked what was happening to hens' eggs that were being incubated in a classroom, most children either drew miniature chicks feeding on food and oxygen, or complete birds just waiting to hatch. However, those children who had had more knowledge and experience of animals reproducing recognised that a process of transformation was taking place (40).

New ideas emerge in a fragile state and as they are tried out and tested they become 'bigger'. The sense that children make of science also depends on their ability to process information – this is dependent on what they know already and their stage of thinking. If children are asked to take on ideas which don't resonate with what they believe, they may memorise what is offered but will continue to hold on to their own ideas to make sense of science-related activities around them.

Children can have very creative ideas to explain scientific happenings, shown, for example, in their responses to questions:

Q: Why does the moon shine?
A: Because the stars sprinkle light on it (girl, 5 years).
Q: What happens to leaves in the winter?
A: They fly away to Australia (boy, 5 years) (41).

These notions are delightfully imaginative but do not help to clarify scientific ideas about the natural world. Fisher agrees:

> Unquestioned, these ideas can hamper the development of truly scientific understanding. Children need to be told, not that their ideas are wrong, but to consider other possibilities and to test them against other theories, to engage in a scientific method of enquiry. Children need to learn to work on their ideas if they are to think scientifically. (42)

A significant step in scientific thinking is moving from describing what is happening to asking why. Fisher suggests that children under seven years are not really interested in why things happen. They just accept a change or sometimes ascribe it to magic.

Case Study 6.6

A reception class and Year 2 class were confronted with an experiment to enquire what happens when cubes of sugar were placed in warm water. The group of five year olds observed that the sugar had simply disappeared into the water and were not aware that any other change had taken place. The seven year olds observed that the sugar had mixed with the water.

Child A: 'But is the sugar still there?'

Child B: 'We would know if the sugar was still there in the water if the water was heavier.'

Teacher: 'How could we test to find out?'

Child B: 'We could do it again but I think that we must do the same things.'

After a lot of discussion the children agreed to repeat the experiment using the same amount of water and weighing the water and tasting it before and after adding the sugar. They found that the addition of sugar had increased the weight and made the water taste sweet.

Child B: 'Well I think that the sugar has made the water heavier and I can taste it [the sugar] so it's there.'

Child A: 'Well, if it's really still there, can we make it come back to be sugar again?'

Child C: 'Let's leave it until tomorrow – maybe the sugar might float to the surface.'

Comment

The five year olds simply concluded that the sugar had disappeared because it was no longer visible. The seven year olds carried out a range of enquiry skills:

- they closely **observed** at each stage of the enquiry
- they **asked questions, made a prediction** and **devised elements of fair testing** to find out more
- they **drew conclusions based on evidence** and **communicated** at each stage of the investigation.

They were interested in the notion of reversibility but had limited understanding of how this might be tested.

Throughout the investigation both groups were intent and absorbed. The teachers had noted the stage of thinking for their groups and planned to extend it:

- to encourage the five year olds to explore and discuss the results of mixing ingredients in cookery lessons
- to introduce scientific words to the seven year olds (dissolve, reverse), encourage them to investigate which materials are reversible, and offer more experiences and discussion of fair testing.

Sharing and sustaining thinking through talk

Children at six and seven years continue to be inquisitive about the world and their expanding language skills mean that they are now more competent to articulate and elaborate their thoughts.

Increased social awareness means that children are now more able to listen to others for longer and offer suitable tailor-made responses. Many of their exchanges and conversations, particularly with peers, are prolonged as they chatter together, toss ideas around, argue, negotiate and acknowledge others' points of view. At times they hesitate or pause, seeming to search for words but then return on track. Language becomes more rational as children learn to make themselves understood by others.

Children process information when they recall what they know and then decide what they wish to share with others. Drawing on previous experiences and a sound understanding of cause and effect, children are now beginning to explain and give reasons for why things happen.

They sometimes question their friends about things that puzzle them and now often follow up their enquiries with supplementary questions. Occasionally children will frame a question as a hypothesis. Simon tentatively suggested to his older brother (hypothesised) that he thought that the sea was salty because of all the seaweed living in it.

In these social and informal situations, where children feel relaxed and unpressurised, on equal ground with the company they keep, they will use language skills which enable them to share and sustain their thoughts.

In other more formal situations they may feel less certain. They become anxious to respond to the expectations of their audience and achieve a correct answer rather than explore and develop their thoughts.

I have observed many examples of these two scenarios and they seem to fit with Barnes' references to 'exploratory' and 'presentational' talk. In the first scenario, children use exploratory talk: some of it is hesitant and incomplete because it enables the speaker to sort out ideas, hear how they sound and see what others make of them. In the second, children are more concerned with demonstrating what they know to an audience (43).

Claxton emphasises these differences when he points out that the child can use talk as a means to frame his thoughts or to create an image of knowing. He suggests that intelligent people need time to find words to say what they want to say. Using a model adopted in counselling, he suggests that talk for creative thinking involves hazy and fragile knowing which indicates growing and organic mindfulness. This he contrasts with talk which does not develop thinking but rather involves leaping to conclusions with confident, 'ready-made and neat' explanations (44).

Further insights into intentional thinking

The early school years is a particularly important stage in children becoming intentional and taking increased control of their thinking. By the time children enter adolescence, capacities for self-regulation are well established.

There is some evidence that aspects of children's capacity for self-regulation has lessened. One study in 2001 replicated a study in the 1940s in which researchers asked children aged three, five and seven years to carry out a number of exercises, including standing perfectly still without moving. They found that: three year olds couldn't do it, five year olds managed it for about three minutes, and seven year olds could stand still for as long as the researchers required. Results from the repeat experiment were different. They showed that the five year olds were acting as three year olds and seven year olds could barely achieve three minutes of stillness (45). Although we recognise that this data is limited to one function, it suggests that today's young children may have less control over their bodies.

Making connections

They become more aware of the power of their mind and how they can use it to understand and solve problems. This ability has developed as a result of early experiences and support in making connections. A child who is not able to forge these links is not in control and simply receives information rather than processing, using and applying it. Feuerstein (quoted in Fisher) believed strongly that all children can improve their thinking 'muscle'. He quotes an example of a girl who needed to take that step. When asked how long it took her to get to school, she had no idea. However, she did know the times of when she caught the bus and when it arrived at school. She also had the calculation skills to arrive at the difference. The girl's difficulty was that her thinking was still fragmented. She was not able to connect the requisite pieces of information to come up with new thinking and solve the problem (46).

Social sensitivity

We have already noted that children between six and seven years are increasingly considerate towards others and much of their thinking relates to belonging in a group. They begin to take part in more activities and hobbies outside school and home, and peer relationships have a greater influence on the way they act and think.

At this age they take greater responsibility for their behaviour and develop standards and expectations for the behaviour of others. This helps them to establish and work within an intentional framework which is noticeable as they increasingly curb impulsive actions, listen, negotiate and collaborate.

Cognitive development

Children also develop a wide range of concepts and skills which provide new areas for them to recognise and develop their sense of self. Seven year-old Anna told me that she was 'a really good reader but rubbish at maths'.

Skills of memory and concentration improve, but this is less likely if children are asked to pay attention, concentrate and remember things in tasks that adults have set. Children will best demonstrate these skills in meaningful situations dealing with experiences that are relevant to them. Moreover, any limitation in attending, memorising and adapting their thinking is not because they are immature or have more limited processing capabilities, but because they don't possess as much experience and expertise as adults. One investigation by Chi and quoted by David Wood showed this clearly. Where separate groups of adults and children were asked to recall random sets of numbers, the adults out-performed the children. However, where the two groups were asked to memorise the positions of chess pieces on a chess board, the children (who were all good chess players) out-performed the adults (who were not experienced in the game) (47).

Practical Activity

Children's capacities to memorise

Observe a group of children who appear to have difficulties memorising and concentrating. Note how well children remember things when:

- asked by the teacher to pay attention and to follow instructions, for example, for keeping the classroom tidy
- asked by another child to pay attention and to follow instructions, for example, carry out steps to make a model
- shown by an adult how to do something, for example, move a cursor on a keyboard to convert text to italics
- shown by an adult how to do something and then helped to remember by working with a 'thinking partner', for example, learn how to play hopscotch
- given oral instructions and then provided with 'memory cards', for example, a card which lays out simple steps to follow in order to write a story
- asked to describe the plot from a favourite story/DVD
- asked to describe the plot with help from a thinking friend.

Consider the reasons for children's different responses and achievements. Use the results from your observations to use the methods which best help to build children's memories.

Metacognition

From around five years, children become more and more aware of how they think and how thinking can be effective. Margaret Donaldson agrees with Vygotsky's view that being aware of thinking is all-important. Donaldson summarises this succinctly: 'If a child is going to control and direct his own thinking, in the kind of way we have been considering, he must become conscious of it' (48).

However, it is not sufficient that children start to think about their thinking, but rather that they use their metacognitive awareness to solve problems. Vygotsky agreed but used a reverse argument, namely that children's use of metacognitive skills is dependent on them having learned them (49). Fisher quotes research into medical practice which suggests that the best doctors are not necessarily the ones who are most knowledgeable, but rather those who know how and when to apply their knowledge. So 'know how' becomes more important than 'know all' (50).

Current primary policy documents in England include aspects of metacognition but do not state the term directly. The document *Excellence and Enjoyment: Learning and Teaching in the Primary Years* recognises development of self-awareness and self-knowledge for learning. Strategies for fostering these competencies are described and include the ability to reflect, self-evaluate and think about their thinking (51). In Wales they have gone further, and produced a series of detailed and helpful guidance documents on children's thinking, and describe metacognition as a central, crucial process in developing skilful thinking (52).

As children mature they begin to recognise strategies to improve their thinking. For example, many three year olds will repeatedly look at an object and touch it in order to remember it (53). Four years later children have developed more strategies to remember things but many do not yet have a realistic view of their capabilities; they tend to overestimate their ability to memorise things and underestimate the effort needed for recall (54).

Metacognitive approaches to dealing with problems

We continually find and face problems in life which we attempt to solve; children have a keen appetite for searching and grappling with problems. The following statement by the National Council of Teachers of Mathematics is not simply restricted to this subject:

> Problem solving is natural to young children because the world is new to them, and they exhibit curiosity, intelligence and flexibility as they face new situations. The challenge at this level is to build on children's innate problem solving inclinations and to preserve and encourage a disposition that values problem solving. (55)

However, regardless of inclination or how much experience and knowledge children have, each problem is in some respects unique and requires a new approach to solving it. Good problem solvers are usually effective thinkers. Although during the early school years some children will still use a trial-and-error approach to solve problems (many adults continue to do so), others will have moved from this *ad hoc* approach to use more intentional ways to resolve problems. An intentional approach requires children to become aware of and use the thinking tools they possess to tackle a dilemma. These include common metacognitive skills of planning, predicting, transferring prior experiences, checking and reflecting. These skills need to be taught and supported (see Chapter 7). Children will then apply their metacognitive knowledge in their own play or in challenging and interesting teacher-directed activity. A small-scale study designed to investigate children's problem-solving knowledge required two five year olds to build block constructions which matched displayed visual models. Both children used some metacognitive knowledge.

- The boy continually monitored his construction by **checking** it against the images; he also demonstrated his building approach to his friends.
- The girl **planned** and **predicted** through self-talk about how she was setting about her building (56).

Children are able to grapple with quite challenging problems if the context is real and of interest to them.

Case Study 6.7

As part of a history project a class of seven year olds were to visit a Norman castle situated seven miles from the school. There was a good ratio of adults to accompany the class. The children responded eagerly to the teacher's suggestion that they should organise the trip. The teacher set up small discussion groups to make decisions about different aspects. Both the teacher and assistant were present during the discussions but the children were responsible for the following decisions.

- They **recalled** a previous visit to a country park and recognised that some of the decisions that the teacher had involved them in were similar to decisions that they needed to make on this occasion.
- They discussed the need to **plan**: what they needed to wear; what they should bring for their lunch; what they needed to find out from the visit.
- Each group identified and **categorised** a list of **questions** to help them with their enquiries. Questions were linked to:
  o reasons for building the castle
  o how it was built
  o the effects of building the castle on the people and the locality.

Comment

In small groups, nearly all the children readily expressed their views, and in most of the groups they listened carefully to each other. A few children recalled their experience of a previous visit and could transfer what they had learned in organising the prospective visit. They recognised the need to plan ahead for the various components of the visit (the most important being where they could purchase an ice cream!). They used enquiry skills and listed very appropriate areas to investigate. Overall children demonstrated very good use of thinking and social skills in dealing with a problem both relevant and personal to them.

Main messages in this chapter

- Children's skill and will to think is marked by their natural capabilities and deep involvement in what interests them.
- Friendships become more important and help children to have regard for other minds, to co-operate and collaborate in shared projects.
- They recall and combine their early stored schema, demonstrate them at different levels and build them into concepts.
- Children's early moves into abstract thinking and understanding of formal symbol systems remain founded on early real experiences and continued opportunities to play around with ideas.
- They share and sustain their thinking through talk, and start to use a wider range of knowledge, skills and concepts which they connect and use intentionally to solve problems.
- When given responsibility, children relish the challenge of problem solving and apply their thinking skills particularly well.

References

1. Robinson, M. (2008) *Child Development from Birth to Eight*. Maidenhead: Open University Press.
2. Lindon, J. (1993) *Child Development from Birth to Eight: A Practical Focus*. London: National Children's Bureau.
3. Fisher, J. (2010) *Moving on to Key Stage 1*. Maidenhead: Open University Press.
4. Green, M. and Palfrey, J.S. (eds) (2001) *Bright Futures, Family Tip Sheets: Middle Childhood*. Arlington, VA: National Centre for Education in Maternal and Child Health.
5. Taggart, G., Ridley, K., Rudd, P. and Benefield, P. (2005) *Thinking Skills in the Early Years – A Literature Review*. Slough: National Foundation for Educational Research (NFER).

6. Claxton, G. (2008) 'Classrooms that Develop Building Power', *NZ Curriculum Online*, 15 November, nzcuriculum.tk.org.nz.
7. Heckhausen, H. (1982), quoted in D. Wood (1998) *How Children Think and Learn*. Oxford: Blackwell, p. 286.
8. Dweck, C.S. (2008) *Mind-set: The New Psychology of Success*. New York: Ballentine Books, p. 7.
9. Robinson, K. (2009) *The Element: How Finding your Passion Changes Everything*. London: Penguin, p. 21.
10. Osborne, E. (1993) *Understanding Your 7 Year Old*. London: Rosendale Press.
11. Hartup, W.W. (1992) *Having Friends, Making Friends, and Keeping Friends: Relationships as Educational Contexts*. Urbana, IL: ERIC Clearinghouse on Elementary and Early Childhood Education, p. 11.
12. Dunn J. (2004) *Children's Friendships: The Beginnings of Intimacy*. Oxford: Blackwell, p. 77.
13. Ibid., p. 4.
14. Helwig, C. and Turiel, E. (2002) 'Children's Social and Moral Reasoning', in P.K. Smith and C.H. Hart (eds), *Blackwell Handbook of Social Development*. Oxford: Blackwell.
15. Ramsey, P.G. (1991) *Making Friends in School*. New York: Teachers College Press.
16. Dunn (2004) *Children's Friendships* (see note 12), p. 54.
17. Ibid., p. 40.
18. Azmitia, M. (1988) 'Peer Interaction and Problem Solving: When Are Two Heads Better than One?', *Child Development*, 59: 87–96.
19. Hartup (1992) *Having Friends, Making Friends, and Keeping Friends* (see note 11).
20. Athey, C. (1990) *Extending Thought in Young Children*. London: Paul Chapman, p. 138.
21. Nuttall, G. (2007) *The Hidden Lives of Learners*. Wellington: New Zealand Council for Educational Research (NZCER), p. 63.
22. Fisher (2010) *Moving on to Key Stage 1* (see note 3), pp. 91–2.
23. Paley, V. (2004) *A Child's Work: The Importance of Fantasy Play*. Chicago, IL, and London: University of Chicago Press, p. 8.
24. Vygotsky, L. (1978) *Mind in Society*. London and Cambridge, MA: Harvard University Press, p. 12.
25. Fisher (2010) *Moving on to Key Stage 1* (see note 3), p. 99.
26. Graham, L. (2004) 'It's Spiderman: Popular Culture in Writing Journals in the Early Years', in *Children's Literacy and Popular Culture*. ESRC Research Seminar Series. Sheffield: University of Sheffield, 11.2.
27. Bruce, T., Meggitt, C. and Grenier, J. (2010) *Child Care and Early Education*. London: Hodder & Stoughton, p. 101.
28. Gurian, M. (2001) *Girls and Boys Learn Differently*. San Francisco, CA: Jossey-Bass.
29. Bodrova, E. and Leong, D.J. (2007) *Tools of the Mind*. Boston, MA: Allyn & Bacon.
30. Anning, A. and Ring, K. (2004) *Making Sense of Children's Drawings*. Maidenhead: Open University Press, p. 118.
31. Bromley, H. (2006) *Making My Own Mark*. London: Early Education, p. 9.
32. Hall, N. (ed.) (1989) *Writing with Reason: The Emergence of Authorship in Young Children*. London: Hodder & Stoughton, p. x.

33. Donaldson, M. (1978) *Young Children's Minds*. London: Fontana Press, p.88.
34. Haylock, D. and Cockburn, A. (2008) *Understanding Mathematics for Young Children*. London: Sage, p. 7.
35. Pound, L. and Lee, T. (2011) *Teaching Mathematics Creatively*. London: Routledge, p. 6.
36. Worthington, M. and Carruthers, E. (2006) *Children's Mathematics: Making Marks, Making Meaning*. London: Sage.
37. Lee, C. (2006) 'Language for Learning Mathematics', cited in Pound and Lee (2011) *Teaching Mathematics Creatively* (see note 35), pp. 42–3.
38. Cheeseman, J. and Monash, B. (2007) 'Young Children's Accounts of their Mathematical Thinking in Essential Research', *Essential Practice*, 11: 192–200. Available at: www.merga.net. av/documents RP132007.
39. Harlen, W. (2009) *The Teaching of Science in Primary Schools* (5th edn). Abingdon: Routledge, p. 71.
40. Ibid., p. 73.
41. Sharp, J., Peacock, G., Johnson, R., Simon, S. and Senath, R. (2002) *Achieving QTS Primary Science: Teaching Theory and Practice*. Exeter: Learning Matters, Chapter 4, p. 60.
42. Fisher, R. (1995) *Teaching Children to Think*. Cheltenham: Stanley Thornes, p. 221.
43. Barnes, D. (2008) 'Introduction', in N. Mercer and S. Hodgkinson (eds), *Exploring Talk in School*. London: Sage.
44. Claxton, G. (2006) 'Thinking at the Edge', *Cambridge Journal of Education*, 36(3), September: 351–62.
45. Spiegel, A. (2008) 'Old-fashioned Play Builds Serious Skills', *National Public Radio*, 21 April.
46. Fisher (1995) *Teaching Children to Think* (see note 42), p. 135.
47. Wood (1998) *How Children Think and Learn* (see note 7), p. 93.
48. Donaldson, M. (1978) *Children's Minds*. Glasgow: Fontana, p. 94.
49. Vygotsky, L. (1968) *Thought and Language*. Cambridge, MA: MIT Press, p. 68.
50. Fisher (1995) *Teaching Children to Think* (see note 42), p. 12.
51. Department for Education and Skills (2004) *Excellence and Enjoyment: Primary National Strategy*. London: DfES, p. 15.
52. Department for Children, Education, Lifelong Learning and Skills (2010) *Why Develop Thinking and Assessment for Learning in the Classroom?* Cardiff: Welsh Assembly Government. Available at: www.wales.gov.uk.
53. Brown, A. and De Loache, J.S. (1983) 'Metacognitive Skills', in M. Donaldson, R. Grieve and C. Pratt (eds), *Early Childhood Development and Education*. Oxford: Blackwell, pp. 280–9.
54. Thornton, S. (2002) *Growing Minds*. Basingstoke: Palgrave Macmillan.
55. National Council of Teachers of Mathematics (NTCM) (2000) *Principles and Standards for School Mathematics*. Reston, VA: NCTM, item 116.
56. Copley, V. and Oto, M. (1997) *An Investigation of Problem Solving Knowledge of a Young Child Doing Block Construction*. Available at: www.west,asu.edu/ cmw/pme/resrepweb/PYC-rr/-copleyntem.

How Close Adults can Support Children's Thinking during the Early School Years

Intentions

This chapter:

- considers how close adults
  - help children to engage in deep interests and strengthen their thinking with others
  - support their move into Key Stage 1
  - enable children to use and sustain talk to think
  - promote meaning-making across subject areas
  - develop the use of higher order skills in intentional thinking

We have made a strong case for the child's initial experiences underpinning all that comes to fruition in the early school years. Of course there will be those children who have had only a narrow range of experiences, those who do not find relationships easy and those who display helpless behaviour. These children will not become good thinkers unless measures are taken to compensate for gaps in their experience and development. They need the rich encounters in play, as described for younger children in previous chapters. They also continue to need a close attachment with a special person. Children cannot be hurried along into thoughtfulness, but given support and time from close adults and peers their thoughts and ideas will grow.

The fortunate children who have had the best possible start to life will enter school as ready, willing and able thinkers. Teachers face the challenge of maintaining these traits for, as Csikszentmihalyi stated, 'the chief impediments to learning are not cognitive in nature. It is not that students cannot learn, it is that they do not wish to' (1).

Relationships

The tremendous changes in society and the virtual disappearance of a close-knit, traditional family life, means that schools are playing an increasingly role in children's social lives. Nevertheless, families in whatever diverse forms continue to matter very much; both close family members and teachers remain crucial to children as thinking companions.

Helping them to find the Element

Children continue to invest all their energies, abilities and enthusiasm when they are involved in experiences and activities that absorb them – when they are in the Element. This implies that, when fostering thinking, parents and teachers need to help each child to find that state.

Ken Robinson suggests that conditions for being in the Element are aptitude and passion, and the features are attitude and opportunity. Teachers, who are the child's special people, can offer support for all four aspects in their role as a thinking companion.

Aptitude
This involves the special person being present and available to children. She will pick up on their interests and talents, and show genuine curiosity in what they are doing (**companionable attention**).

Passion
Once the special person notes a child's aptitude, she will give him attention, work with him as a co-player and thinker and encourage him to deepen his interests and practice and apply what he knows. She will recognise when he is working at a deep level of involvement and try to protect these times (**companionable play**).

Attitude
Robinson suggests that how we see our circumstances and how we recognise and seize opportunities is linked closely to what we expect of ourselves (2). Children who have optimistic and positive attitudes have a growth mind-set (see Chapter 4). They are learning to cope with frustrations, set-backs and hindrances. Others are less resilient; when things go wrong their thinking is blocked by feelings of failure. The special person needs to help all children develop 'I can' traits by:

- keeping an eye on a child's work, anticipating when he may face a hurdle and being available to offer advice, for example, with an unstable construction, or a piece of writing which has no sequence or structure
- urging a child to focus on the processes of his work rather than only concentrating on the product
- suggesting that the child thinks about and describes his problem; sometimes, by reflecting and talking about it, he may begin to see a way through
- offering practical assistance, for example, following the child's instructions to build a den
- encouraging children to understand that making a mistake/taking a wrong decision can be very useful if we learn something from it
- sharing her own experiences of set-backs and disappointments in daily life (a failed cake, plants in the garden eaten by slugs) and how she dealt with them (persevered in making another cake, grew more plants and put down slug repellent).

This support is offered through shared talk in **companionable conversations**.

Opportunity

Before they start school most children will have many and diverse experiences, some of which may have touched them profoundly and influenced their own interests.

Case Study 7.1

Lukas's dad Nikola was a painter and decorator. During school holidays he invited his five year old son to accompany him on work visits and to help. At first this meant simply watching carefully what his dad did, carrying some materials and clearing things away. Nikola explained what he was doing as he worked and Lukas became knowledgeable about the different processes involved in decorating. At home he was allowed to help his dad decorate a wall in his bedroom.

This was the start of Lukas's passion. As Nikola gave him a little more responsibility, showing him how to mix up the paint, so Lukas gained confidence and became proficient. In school, he talked enthusiastically about his ambition to become a proper decorator. He relished aspects of mathematics when his teacher explained the need for mathematical skills in his future trade. Three years later he produced a sustained piece of work showing detailed plans and calculations involved in decorating a room in the flat where he lived with his family.

Comment

Nikola was instrumental in providing an opportunity for Lukas to develop an interest and become proficient in exercising it:

> - He made visible the different aspects of his work and helped his son to understand the reasons for each process.
> - He trusted Lukas to take responsibility but remained close as the senior working partner and helped him to progress in guided participation.
>
> Lukas's teachers picked up on his interest acquired in the home and used this to motivate him in learning mathematics and later to apply his knowledge and thinking in a self-chosen project.

There remain other children who have not had the encounters enjoyed by Lukas, nor have they had the benefit of being with a person like Nikola to help them recognise and grow their talents. In school, the child's special person is in a strong position to open all children's eyes to the possibilities of gaining different interests, having new ideas and moving up the exciting spiral of finding their Element. She can:

- arrange for visiting experts, including family members, to visit to demonstrate their skills and share their enthusiasms, for example, musicians, artists, potters, gardeners, carpenters
- ensure that the visiting experts make clear how they came to find their Element and how to keep hold of it, for example, through perseverance, practice and sharing with like-minded people
- organise visits to places which show evidence of great achievements, for example, an art gallery, an allotment, a suitable concert, a cathedral.

Teachers and parents can also influence children to find the Element through the models they offer. Writing in the *Journal of the Royal Society of Arts*, James Flynn suggests that children can begin to grow their own rich mental environment:

the things that parents do at present for their children are all worth doing; reading stories, good diet and exercise, good schooling. But somewhere along the line children must fall in love with ideas ... so they will ... seek out friends who are alert, earn their living doing something cognitively complex, develop leisure interests that are challenging. And the best way to get them to fall in love with ideas is to fall in love with ideas yourselves. (3)

Lillian Katz echoes this:

If teachers want their young pupils to have robust dispositions to investigate, hypothesise, experiment, conjecture and so forth, they might consider making their own such intellectual dispositions more visible to the children. (4)

Case Study 7.2

Mikey (six years) was in an infant school which allotted generous time for children to select their own experiences and activities. On these occasions Mikey returned again and again, always alone, to the mark-making table where he drew very detailed diagrams of bikes and motorbikes. Sometimes he labelled parts of the bike and at other times he was keen to describe how the machine worked.

Jen, his teacher, observed three or four children in turn over a week to find out how they spent their self-chosen time. She quickly noted Mikey's interest and aptitude. In conversation with him, she found out that he liked drawing at home and that drawing machines was his very favourite thing in school. From then on Jen and her assistant followed Mikey's work and encouraged him when he was frustrated (he stormed around when he could not translate his mental image of a particular machine on to paper). The following week, Jen brought her own mountain bike into the classroom. She talked to the children about her interest in mountain biking, and explained how the various mechanisms worked on the bike. Jen invited children to explore the bike and to represent it in drawings, writing, model-making through photography. Until then Mikey's work was derived from his imagination and he relished a new challenge, sharing his many thoughts and ideas about machines with other interested children.

Comment

Jen had made good provision for Mikey to find his Element:

- She resourced a rich environment inside and out and allotted two hours daily for children to select experiences that interested them.
- She gave time to observe and talk to children, found out about and showed interest in Mikey's passion and talent.
- She encouraged him to persevere and maintain a positive attitude during periods of frustration.
- She provided for further challenges by sharing her own interest and offering Mikey a new opportunity to draw from observation, offer support and learn from others.

Links with Parents

How do you find out about children's particular interests at home?
How much do parents know about their child's interests and talents in school?
How do you weave children's home interests into the school programme?

Opportunities for thinking in social groups

The significance of children's friendships was outlined in the previous chapter. From 5–7 years onwards, children increasingly find strength in friendships and in these intimate relationships they share thoughts and ideas both informally and in lessons. As relationships become more stable, teachers increasingly recognise the potential of friendship groups to aid children's sustained, shared thinking. The following practices are helpful.

Introduce thinking friends

This is a slightly different take on *Talking partners* – a useful strategy to encourage children to converse with each other. This approach encourages children to select their own partner/friend and to focus on helping each other to think well. It works particularly well with mature, older children who work easily with others.

- Ask children to 'consider others in the class who have good ideas, are interested in your thoughts, share their thoughts with you, and spark off your own thinking'.
- Suggest that they choose one child to approach and ask them if they would become their 'thinking friend' ('thinking friends' are often selected from established friendship groups).
- Explain to the children that their (new) friend is available to work with them during self-chosen activities and in class and small-group discussion times. By thinking together (stress that both parties should gain) their ideas will expand.
- Trial and monitor the arrangement initially for a week and ask the thinking partners to share with others how well they think it is working.
- Ask questions to help both parties evaluate:
  - how well did your thinking friend listen to you and accept your ideas?
  - how did he explain if he did not agree with your thoughts?
  - how did your friend develop/add to your ideas?
  - how well does the arrangement for thinking friends work for you?
  - how could it be more useful?

Supporting children's transitions into Key Stage 1

Although during their early years most children will have experienced various transitions from home to different settings, the move into Key Stage 1 can be the most problematic. (Wales sensibly defer this move until seven years.) We have seen in the previous chapter that children's development from 5–7 years does not change dramatically; likewise, the ways in which they think and learn best remain through first-hand and self-chosen experiences with a special person acting as a thinking companion. And yet, as they move into Year 1 at five and six years of age many are expected to comply with a different curriculum which is more prescribed and controlled by the teacher. Fisher provides a very useful list of differences between practice in many Reception and Year 1 classes, identified by a range of teachers (5).

The greater the gap between the cultures of the EYFS and Key Stage 1, the greater the challenge for the child, and the greater the risk of jeopardising their early competencies in becoming strong and effective thinkers. The good news is that some schools are increasingly developing Year 1 practice to align more closely with developmentally appropriate practice in Reception classes. This enlightened approach is endorsed in the Tickell Report, where Reception and Year 1 teachers are recommended to work closely together (6). Nevertheless, at the time of writing, this is not common custom.

The following practices are helpful to smooth transition:

- Become aware of children's thoughts about the prospective transition.
  - Ask parents to share: any comments (positive and negative) their child makes about the forthcoming move; any different behaviour – sleeplessness, irritability. These insights can help you to plan actions to deal with any concerns.
  - In small groups, ask children to share their views on the forthcoming move.
- Plan the transition over a year.
  - In the summer term, Year 1 teachers visit Reception to observe how the children they will receive are supported to think effectively and intentionally (the foundation for Year 1).
  - In the autumn term, Reception teachers visit their former children now in Year 1 to observe how their thinking competencies are developing.
- Ensure that children are reassured by the familiar. A national training programme, *Continuing the Learning Journey* (7), posed some useful questions which can highlight the differences that children may confront in their move. These are helpful for the Reception and Year 1 teacher to consider together.
  - What do the children see that is the same in Year 1 and in Reception?
  - What do children experience that is the same in Year 1 and in Reception?
  - What do children encounter both in Year 1 and in Reception?
- Aim for each child to move into their new class with a friend and, where possible, arrange for their school pegs to be located next to each other.

- Connect with knowledge and interests that the child brings from home and his previous class.
  - Each child chooses one piece of work completed in Reception (painting, drawing, piece of writing, model) that he would like to take into Year 1. These are displayed in Year 1 on the first day of term. Children are encouraged to discuss them and share them with their new teachers.
- Involve parents in planning for the transition.

Case Study 7.3

One school produced a DVD entitled *Welcome to Year 1*, filmed and narrated by children. It included photographs of the Year 1 staff, features of the classroom and outside area, and a sequence of routine daily events. The DVD ended with some questions directed to children's viewing:

- Has this DVD helped you to know more about moving into Year 1?
- What do you like best about the Year 1 classroom?
- What sort of books might you choose from the book area?
- What new things are you looking forward to learning and doing?

Each family with a child in the reception class received a copy. Parents were asked to view the DVD on several occasions with their child (and continue to play it until the child lost interest). Stress was placed on the importance of shared viewing, listening to the child's comments and questions, and sharing a conversation about the transition.

Comment

All parents were very positive about the DVD and most appeared to take an active role in viewing and discussing it with their children. In a follow-up meeting designed to evaluate the impact, 30 (out of a possible 50) families attended. They reported that the DVD had helped to:

- inform and reassure their children, most importantly about what happened in the classroom every day
- open up the topic of transition and reveal individual children's thoughts, concerns and additional questions, for example, 'Will my new teacher be cross if I get things wrong?'
- inform parents and give them an important role in aiding the transition.

All of the reception children had reportedly asked to view the DVD again and again, and referred to it when they started in their new class. Positive comments from Year 1 children suggested that the resource appeared to have provided them with useful information which helped them manage the entry into their new class. Teachers met with parents and children to discuss what more could have been done to ease the transition.

Communication and companionship

We noted previously (see Chapter 5) some limitations in adults questioning children where:

- children only give brief or one-word answers
- they direct the answer only to the practitioner
- the practitioner controls the session.

This can easily occur when exploring stories with a group and focusing on children's recall. Questioning rituals can focus on 'What happened next?', and 'Then what happened?' or 'Who did what, and who ran into the garden?' (8). These rituals usually mean that the teacher dominates the talk and the children say very little, being required to simply report on what they remember. A teacher who is a thinking companion recognises that a different approach is needed, understanding the importance of children using talk to share, extend and sustain their thinking with others. She will offer:

- **Companionable attention:** Have close regard to what children are trying to convey in their conversations with each other. Often quiet children who do not contribute much are deeply engaged and their occasional contributions can be thoughtful and incisive. Attention can simply mean unobtrusive listening on the side-line but, importantly, children know that their special person is interested and this helps to validate what they are saying.
- **Companionable conversations:** Although talk in school is increasingly planned and managed as a valuable tool to promote thinking, time still needs to be set aside for friendly, reciprocal and informal exchanges with individuals and groups. Such human conversations cement relationships with children and may give clues to what really matters to them.
- **Companionable play:** Children at six and seven years are becoming experienced players and enjoy opportunities to plan and carry out play projects with their friends. At this stage the adult's role changes. Fisher describes her observations of children playing at Key Stage 1 and noted that children tended to depend on other children rather than the adult. She suggests that now, rather than taking the initiative, the adult needs to wait to be invited into a play bout and become involved on the child's terms (9). This different emphasis requires: close observation of children in order to gauge how self-sufficient they are in play; a watchful eye for any signal that the teacher is welcome to join the group (a direct request to take a role, respond to a question, provide an extra resource); and sensitivity in not over-staying her welcome!

- **Companionable apprenticeship:** If children have already had good experiences of working alongside adults and their peers, they will now recognise what they can gain from guided participation. Children may learn:
  - o cause and effect from a more informed child. This may be demonstrated very simply through direct instruction. 'Look, listen, Ibu' said Ben. 'If you turn this knob on the overhead projector you can make that toy look smaller or bigger.'
  - o to expand their vocabulary of 'thinking words'. These may be modelled by an adult using words such as 'know', 'guess', 'remember', 'understand', 'repeat'.

Climate

Support meaning-making

In making sense, children aged 5–7 years still need access to plenty of real things and events. The opportunities to have, repeat and discuss these direct experiences provide the means for them to replay them in their head – moving on to abstract thought. The move into Key Stage 1 is the interface between experiential and symbolic thinking.

Discrete and infused methods of teaching thinking across the National Curriculum

Children need not only to be made aware of different ways of thinking but must practise using them so that they become internalised and are used in problem solving. Carol McGuiness usefully distinguishes between discrete and infused methods (see Chapter 1) (10). She suggests that discrete methods draw on particular materials to promote thinking and infused methods rely on daily practice which provokes and supports children to think. These methods are outlined below.

Discrete methods
Methods using sessions of 'dialogic talk' and 'philosophy for children' provide scope for children to use thinking skills as tools to help them investigate and solve problems with others.

Dialogic talk
Robin Alexander makes the important point that 'Talk in learning is not a one-way linear communication but a reciprocal process in which ideas are bounced back and forth and on that basis take children's thinking forward' (11). Promoting dialogue differs from the easy, unstructured conversations that are used with young children or the more limited

question-and-answer approach described earlier in the chapter. The method is described in a government document.

> Teaching through dialogue enables teachers and pupils to share and build on ideas in sustained talk. ... Teachers encourage children to listen to each other, share ideas and consider alternatives; build on their own and each other's ideas to develop coherent thinking; express their views fully and help each other to reach common understandings. Teaching through dialogue can take place when a teacher talks with an individual pupil, or two pupils are talking together, or when the whole class is joining in discussion. (12)

Dialogue does not happen spontaneously. Children need to understand how to contribute their ideas and learn from the ideas of others. The ground will have been laid if children are used to discussion with talking partners or thinking friends and they have been encouraged from an early age to share their ideas. They now need to learn how to talk and think effectively in groups. Dawes reminds us that 'children may not be aware that the best use of speaking and listening is as a tool for exploring one another's ideas, or to reason together' (13). Children in the early years of school can start to develop this awareness and practise it in group dialogue, for example by being encouraged to ask questions.

Children usually are enthusiastic about group work. A group of children in the Reggio schools were clear about the benefits, which they suggested should include: the fun of doing things together; enabling your brain to work better; and sharing ideas to make a big one (14).

Teachers can support dialogic talk by:

- initially structuring small groups to include some confident children who may model talk and thinking to others. As they become more experienced, children can choose who they work with.
- establishing rules for talking and thinking together in groups. These should be negotiated with children until they agree a list. In the example below, a Year 2 teacher devised an initial list and asked for additional suggestions from the group.

Teacher's list:

- make your thoughts clear to one another
- be prepared to be questioned or asked to explain what you mean
- listen carefully to a different view
- try to come to some agreement.

Children's list:

- only one person speaks at a time
- if you don't agree with something, you must give a reason.

The joint list was ratified, displayed in class and referred to at the beginning of all joint sessions.

Case Study 7.4

Sean, Ed and Den (seven years) had listened carefully to the topic in assembly which was about children less fortunate than them, who were hungry, poorly clothed and did not have proper accommodation. Back in class, their teacher invited them to think in small groups about the messages they had just heard.

Den: 'Well, what I want to know is really why are some people hungry in the world?'

Sean: 'Well, see they haven't got money, and well it's because they won't work. If you don't work you can't have money to buy food.'

Ed: 'No, that's not right, it's not right.'

Teacher: 'Well, what do you think is the reason, Ed?'

Ed: 'I dunno, perhaps, perhaps their dads haven't got work.'

Sean: 'Well, my dad and my mum work – that's why I'm not hungry … see.'

Den: 'Well, I know that, but my dad, my dad says there's not enough jobs to go round.' [Pauses]

Ed: 'Right, my dad and my sister, they ent got jobs, they can't find a job.'

Den: 'Listen Sean, if your dad only had half a job he could give the other half to someone else – that's fair.'

Sean: 'I, I don't know – if, if my dad had only got half a job what else would he do? He don't like lying in bed.'

Den: 'I know, perhaps he could help other people to only do half a job – that would mean that more people get another half. That would be ace, wouldn't it?'

Sean: 'Yeh, but you can't [do that]. You need a law to do that.'

Comment

The boys were reflective and deeply engaged in a sustained conversation. They were able to tackle challenging subjects of money and employment as these were issues that concerned two of the boys' families. Some contributions are hesitant as they search for words to describe their thoughts. They listened to each other and Den and Ed challenged Sean's suggestion. There was some tension between their shared thoughts which led to the emergence of a new idea. This exchange fulfils most of the agreed criteria for talking and thinking together, although there was no agreed resolution.

- Encourage exploratory talk. This type of talk enables children to try out their ideas, using words such as 'you know', 'maybe', 'might'. They also justify their ideas, using 'because'. Exploratory talk is shared with others and Sean and Den (Case Study 7.4) used this conversational ploy to explore one another's ideas. This type of talk will develop when the teacher explains that:
  - o thinking out loud is a way of making our thoughts clear to ourselves
  - o talking with others helps to share thoughts and ideas
  - o sometimes it's difficult to find the words to describe our thoughts but others in the group are there to help us.

The teacher:

- makes clear at the start of a group session that the aim is for children to think together, consider and add to the thoughts of others in the group
- allows unrushed time for children to play around with thoughts and words
- offers encouragement, for example, 'I think that I understand you, Delia, that's a very interesting idea. Can you explain a little more about it?'
- builds in regular opportunities for rehearsal: the more opportunities that children have to talk their thoughts out loud, the more able they become to articulate them.

Philosophy for children

This approach uses what children have learned in dialogic talk to help them consider puzzling issues. It is founded on the importance of philosophical inquiry, critical thinking and dialogue (15, 16). It supports the development of a 'Community of Enquiry', where children sit in a circle with a close adult and consider philosophical and puzzling questions to which there is no one right answer. The sessions are managed by the adult, who supports children to share their ideas and views and struggle with the ideas that others offer. Moreover, acting as a thinking companion, the adult also contributes to the discussion and occasionally asks questions as an equal member of the group. Although dialogic talk and philosophy for children both support children's thinking and promote similar ground-rules for speaking and listening, the former method encourages small-group work while philosophy sessions usually engage the whole class in discussion.

Developing this approach requires the adult to be conversant with the principles and practicalities of managing the session and these details are listed in manuals in the reference section (17, 18).

Teachers will develop effective thinking using philosophy for children sessions by:

- ensuring that children have good social skills to work easily with one another
- presenting interesting stimulus which engage children (from stories, film, artefacts, current affairs)
- encouraging children to hold their own views and feel confident to share them with others.

In an open letter to *The Guardian*, many eminent authors, scientists and philosophers proposed that 'introducing philosophy lessons in the classroom from a very early age would have immense benefits in terms of boosting British schoolchildren's reasoning and conceptual skills, and better equipping them for the complexities of life in the 21st century' (19).

Infused methods

Carol McGuiness introduced 'Activating Children's Thinking Skills (ACTS)' as a framework of thinking processes and strategies which can be infused and permeate across the curriculum. McGuiness found that the benefits of this approach are:

- matching thinking skills directly with curriculum topics
- livening up teaching methods and promoting pupil's deeper understanding
- using learning and teaching time well
- supporting teaching for thoughtfulness across subjects
- helping the transfer and re-enforcement of learning (20).

The ACTS project is designed for use by 8–12 year olds but the approach, suitably adapted, is applicable for younger children. Teachers need to be aware of the teaching processes that they will weave into subject content. The list below (adapted from the ACTS materials) provides a reasonable agenda but is not exhaustive.

Some types of thinking

- Information processing – sorting, sequencing, planning, classifying, grouping information
- Analysing – examining parts of a problem and how they fit into the whole, comparing/contrasting, distinguishing fact from opinion
- Reasoning – drawing on current knowledge, rearranging it and applying it to new issues, giving reasons for a point of view and seeing cause and effect

(Continued)

(Continued)

- Enquiring – the process of finding out, including asking relevant questions
- Creating – generating and connecting ideas, imagining or hypothesising, coming up with imaginative solutions
- Evaluating – reflecting and considering, developing ways of judging the value of ideas and information, relating causes and effects, designing a fair test

Other processes which support thinking

- Empathy – recognising and appreciating others' ideas and points of view
- Expression – rehearsing and clarifying thoughts, views and ideas in order to share with and present to others

Table 7.1 is helpful for raising awareness of where there is scope for children to use some thinking processes in different subjects. A similar chart could be devised which refers to the seven areas of learning and is relevant for children in the Reception class.

Table 7.1   Examples of Infusing Types of Thinking into Subject Areas

Scope in Subjects	Information processing	Analysing	Reasoning	Enquiring	Creating	Evaluating
English						
Mathematics						
Science						
Information and Communication Technology						
Geography						
History						
Art and Design						
Religious Education						
PHSE and Citizenship						

Pedagogy to support thinking across subject areas

Infusing thinking is essentially about good teaching, where adults:

- plan and highlight where specific teaching skills can be woven into subject content
- pick up on child-initiated learning, referring to children's ideas and provoking further thinking
- develop dialogue using daily events
- use exciting classroom projects to motivate and challenge children's thinking (see Case Study 7.5 below).

Infusing thinking skills in different areas and subjects

Thinking skills must be introduced in a context so that children can recognise how they can use different thinking tools to achieve different purposes.

Support thinking in writing

Composing in writing involves creative thought, generating ideas and imagining (what will happen to whom, when and where), and expressive thought, planning and presenting the sequence of events. Many thoughts and ideas derived in play may be channelled into imaginative writing. The early findings of a research project on creative writing show that children in nursery and Key Stage 1 years 'were markedly more enthusiastic about writing than older children about their writing' (21). Mallett, referring to Palmer, suggests that one important reason for this, confirming what all experienced practitioners know, is that role play offers strong and imaginative contexts for writing. Setting writing in play:

> help[s] children to see the purpose and audience for their efforts, and because they are usually very keen to convey their thoughts, the efforts involved in writing seem worthwhile. (22)

Teachers can support creative thinking for writing by:

- providing a rich resource of stories to feed the imagination
- planning for and provoking children to engage together in episodes of fantasy
- encouraging composition and re-enactment of familiar stories, where children introduce different events. 'After the ball the prince visited Cinderella's house and decided that he didn't want to marry her after all because she was dressed in rags'.

- offering 'what if' scenarios to think about. Provide the end of a story and ask them to discuss the events leading up to it. 'The tiger roamed in the mountains never giving up the search for his wife.'
- providing children with 'ideas books' and suggest that they jot down ideas that pop into their heads during the day; encourage the use of diagrams and pictures as well as notes to capture ideas. They may also store these electronically.

Non-fiction writing helps children to organise their thoughts, for example making lists. Children need to recognise the purpose of lists in planning what to purchase or what to do. When starting an investigation, for example considering what they want to find out, children can be encouraged to list their enquiries. Mallett describes a lovely example of how children keep 'wonder books' where they list all the things that they want to find out. She suggests that 'this kind of list leads to genuine interests and the burgeoning of hobbies' (23).

One study of children in Years 1 and 2 (reported in an NFER report) investigated how well they could express an argument in writing. The children used 'writing frames' which showed the structures used in making arguments. In Year 1 the challenge was a book about zoos that contests children's uncritical response to them. Year 2 children interviewed a visitor who educated his children at home. Following these provocations, children discussed as a class and came up with 'for and against' arguments. The authors concluded that the children 'are able intellectually, to grasp the complexity of an issue and can develop an argument following the conventions of the discourse in a sophisticated way' (24).

Practical Activity

Comparing and contrasting texts

Read two different accounts of a well-known folk tale, for example, the traditional tale of *The Three Little Pigs* and *The True Story of the 3 Little Pigs* by Jon Scienszka and Lane Smith. Provide copies of both books for children to share in small groups (for them to refer to rather than read).

Ask the groups to discuss the different accounts, suggest which they think is the true version and try to give their reasons. Encourage groups in turn to present their views to the class. Ask each group to consider if what they have heard from others has changed their judgements.

Support thinking in mathematics

We have already explored the breadth of learning in mathematics. Pound and Lee passionately endorse the importance of creative approaches in teaching the subject, arguing that this can enthuse children and also help them move from being dependent on concrete experiences to using symbols (25).

Case Study 6.7 (in the previous chapter), which was based on a historical enquiry, has considerable scope for children's mathematical thinking. For example:

- gathering information about the programme and overall timing of the day, such as times allocated for touring the castle and grounds, toilet and lunch stops (information processing)
- estimating the length of the journey based on the distance travelled and problems with traffic (information processing, making connections, reasoning based on past experiences)
- reflecting after the visit on the effectiveness of the visit and the accuracy of the timing. What could have been improved? (evaluating)

Support thinking in science

Wynne Harlen suggests that children's scientific ideas, based on their early experiences, are adapted and adjusted through enquiry. She identifies how, through enquiry, children's initial ideas can:

- be developed into bigger ideas
- move from description to explanation
- progress from individual to shared ideas.

Harlen and Qualter quote a case study of Year 1 children who worked on a problem that they enjoyed presenting through a story, followed by a question about choosing a bouncy ball for a dog. Children examined various balls and, based on their experiences, made **predictions** about their 'bounciness'. The teacher challenged their predictions, asking 'How do you know?'. This led to **an investigation**, where the balls were tested, and they **compared** the evidence collected with their original predictions. Finally, a number of balls were selected to be tested further. Throughout the lesson the teacher took photographs of each stage of the process (26).

Important features of the lesson included opportunities to play around with the balls and to develop their thinking though shared talk. The photographs served as a record of the enquiry and meant that children were not burdened with writing.

This lesson allowed children to move from:

- having their own experiences of using balls to develop a **bigger idea** about the bounciness of balls in general

- **describing** the balls to **explaining** why some were 'bouncier'
- having their own ideas to **sharing their ideas** through working in pairs and small groups.

All of these examples of infused practice arise from identifying and planning support for different forms of thinking which arise in specific subjects. The examples are also founded on providing children with enjoyable and interesting content to motivate their thoughts and ideas. A further approach uses topics or projects based on children's interests and which exploit natural links between subjects. This offers a more holistic approach to learning.

Infusing thinking through project work

Case Study 7.5

Children Thinking at Key Stage 1

At Trimdon Grange nursery and infant school in the North of England the head teacher decided to build the Key Stage 1 curriculum based on children's interests. She asked the children what they had most enjoyed during their time in the Reception class and came up with their three priorities.
  The children had really liked:

- working with people (not teachers) who had real expertise
- using real tools (woodwork and design technology tools)
- working on large-scale projects.

The head and staff based the curriculum on cross-curricular themes which responded to these interests. They:

- found ways to bring in expertise from within the community, including parents and grandparents
- provided a working area where children could work with different tools and learn to master a variety of practical techniques
- planned large-scale, collaborative events which required working in a variety of scales (planning and participating in a local carnival).

  Years 1 and 2 children follow a two-year rolling programme which is based on motivating projects, for example, devising a go-cart race involving groups of children building their own go-cart. In this project the children worked and talked together in small groups, used a variety of tools in the process of construction and gained from expertise from visiting experts (an engineer and a carpenter). The task was carefully cross-referenced to aspects of the National Curriculum Programmes of Study in mathematics, science, communication, design and information technology.

The thinking processes involved in the project included:

- gathering information about the task in hand (information processing)
- drawing on and using their personal knowledge in developing the go-cart (reasoning)
- recognising how discrete aspects of the task contribute to the final product (analysing)
- sharing, connecting and refining ideas (creative)
- finding out new information through reading, surfing the web and asking questions (inquiring)
- recognising ways of fair testing their go-carts, understanding reasons for strengths and weaknesses, reflecting on the effectiveness of their machines (evaluating).

The project offered great scope for children to work independently but the adults, both teachers and family members, played a strong role as thinking companions.

This is one example of outstanding practice in a school where there is great scope for children to think, the integrity of the National Curriculum is maintained and standards of achievement are high.

Figure 7.1

Sustaining intentional thinking

Children aged 4–7 years become increasingly aware of themselves as thinkers and learners, and develop metacognitive skills. Istomina provides an example when studying the ways that different age groups respond to a directed shopping task using a class shop. The four year olds ran to and fro 'purchasing things' that they could remember. The five and six year olds tried to remember what they had been told by asking for the instructions to be repeated. The seven year olds tried to make some rational connections between items on their list (27).

The provision suggested in Chapter 5 to support intentionality and self-regulation should be sustained in Years 1 and 2. This continuity will encourage those children who need more time to develop as confident and reflective thinkers to recognise and use their thinking capabilities deliberately to solve problems.

While good practice continues to provide a climate, management style and environment to promote thinking for all children, some will be ready for further challenges, thinking about their thinking in more depth.

Teachers need to:

- work with children bearing in mind their different levels of metacognitive awareness
- ensure that children are familiar with and know when to use different thinking processes
- plan and develop ways to help children reflect on and assess their thinking
- develop a classroom climate environment which supports metacognition
- directly model metacognitive behaviour.

Bear in mind children's different levels of metacognitive awareness

Professional checkpoint

Recognise where your children are

One study suggests that children increase their levels of awareness in metacognitive thinking through the ways in which they make decisions (28). Identify your children's levels of awareness through matching their decision-making approaches to these statements:

- Tacit use of thinking: children make decisions spontaneously, without thinking about them
- Aware use: children become consciously aware of a strategy or decision-making process
- Strategic use: children organise their thinking by selecting strategies for decision-making
- Reflective use: children reflect on thinking, before, during and after the process, pondering on progress and how to improve.

Larkin suggests that gifted children may have greater metacognitive capacities. She refers to some characteristics of giftedness taken from the National Association for Gifted Children, namely that the child:

- understands and makes abstractions earlier: may ignore details
- is quick to recognise relationships, including cause and effect; may have difficulty in accepting illogicality
- evaluates facts, arguments and people critically, including themselves.

Larkin claims that these criteria also apply to metacognitive behaviour (29).

Teachers can help children to start to achieve these indicators by:

- encouraging them to recognise and focus on the 'big picture' (the whole) and identify the key features (the component parts that make up the whole). Children need to ask themselves 'So what are we trying to solve? What is the main problem? What is involved in the problem?' (analysing)
- helping them to connect and use plausible former knowledge to enlighten their efforts in unravelling a new problem (reasoning)
- showing them how to weigh up the information given and arguments presented, distinguishing between belief, opinion and fact (evaluating).

Case Study 7.6

An inquiry

The teacher adapted a problem-solving model to provide a sequence and structure for children's thinking. She asked the children to suggest something in the school that they wanted to do and find out more about. The children decided that they wanted to know how to develop their school garden (the big picture):

(Continued)

(Continued)

- children contributed all that they knew about gardens (information processing)
- children brainstormed what they needed to find out in order to tackle this enquiry (size of plot, type of soil, shelter, sun/shade, comparing suitable plants and types of paths) (analysing)
- they discussed how they would find this information (the questions they would ask, information, books and websites they would access) (inquiring)
- they shared ideas about what they wanted the garden to be and look like (imagining, generating ideas)
- working in small groups, they shared ideas and agreed the best ones, weighing up what was realistic and within the budget that was available (evaluating)
- they drew up a critical path of action to help them achieve their aim (planning).

Comment

The teacher introduced each stage of the enquiry. She encouraged the children to suggest the types of thinking they would need for each stage, and where they were unsure she rehearsed with them each of the thinking processes. She ensured that the children remained focused but otherwise maintained a low profile.

Ensure that children are familiar with and know when to use different thinking processes

Guidance from Wales suggests that teachers and children need to share a vocabulary which will help them to talk about thinking processes (see the list in the box below which indicates a progression in use of terms) (30).

Talking about thinking: a suggested vocabulary

- plan, develop, reflect
- thinking time, suggest ideas, brainstorm
- explore success criteria, improve, evaluate criteria
- sort, group, sequence, classify
- similarities and differences, compare, pros and cons, seeking patterns
- cause and effect, reason, predict
- work it out, conclude, justify, evaluate
- guess, weigh up, imagine, estimate, make inferences, speculate, analyse
- question, decide, discuss solutions, summarise outcomes

- opinions, bias, reliability
- consider, choose, model, monitor, review, learning/thinking strategy, reflect, metacognition
- make links, make connections, relationships.

Links with Parents

Encourage parents to give their children scope to use a range of thinking skills in everyday situations at home, for example using the context of a birthday party:

- plan and help to select food for their party
- plan and organise the sequence of party games, recognising that one of the invited children uses a wheelchair
- reflect on the best parts of the party – what would they like to do again next year and what could have been better?

Plan and develop ways to help children to reflect on and assess their thinking

A Welsh guidance document makes clear that if teaching is to be effective, assessment needs to be firmly aligned with learning (and thinking). This involves helping children to learn how to learn (and think) (31). Assessment for learning (and thinking) is central to children becoming self-regulating and understanding how they might become better thinkers.

Encourage children to reflect on their thinking

Reflection is at the heart of metacognition and it should be ongoing. There is still a tendency to cram reflection time into a plenary session which allows little opportunity for a child to ruminate on his thoughts, ideas and actions, and when time is short simply reduces his contribution to a statement of his action. Reflection does not come easily to children at this age, but with practice, time and encouragement from an interested audience the skill will develop.

Questioning children can provoke them to reflect on their thinking. Rather than appear to interrogate, it is important that questions should be offered in the spirit of friendly interest. The following questions are helpful:

- Which types of thinking did you use most?
- Which other sorts of thinking might you have used?
- What new thoughts did you use from others?
- How helpful was it to talk to yourself about your thinking?

Teachers know their children well and will recognise if these questions are too challenging or if they need to adapt their language to make the questions more accessible.

Help children to become familiar with ways to assess their thinking

Children need to understand the criteria or requirements for achieving higher level thinking. This is difficult for children of this age but the teacher can help by pointing out the following steps in progress. For example:

- posing a key question which encourages further thinking
- pursuing an enquiry by asking supplementary questions
- deliberately using a thinking strategy for a particular purpose
- recognising and making a connection between two ideas.

As more mature children become familiar with these steps in progress, they will begin to identify them when working with peers.

Plan opportunities for peer assessment

Assessment with peers is really helpful as the relationship is equal and children are more likely to feel relaxed. They will take heed of comments and criticism from other children and are more inclined to interrupt and ask questions.

However, peer assessment will only be successful if children have been used to working collaboratively, for example, as talking partners, thinking friends and through dialogic talk. Although most children will relish working together, some will still need support in the basic skills of conversation, listening, attending and keeping to an agenda.

It is important that the teacher is clear about her role. She will set the parameters for thinking together but she should not be obtrusive. By listening in to discussions she may help to clarify a point, ask a child to pursue a question and help children to work out how well their peers have achieved in their thinking. This is challenging for children at six and seven years but it is the progress in thinking processes that is important.

Develop a classroom environment and climate which supports metacognition

The displayed environment should give a high priority to listing different thinking processes, helping children to recognise the language of thinking and provoking children to think in different ways.

Highlight different thinking processes:

- Children need to be introduced to different ways of thinking and will be reminded of them by referring to displays. A visual display will help them to use and apply thinking processes in other contexts.
- Display a board of 'thinking words' and highlight a thinking word of the week. Encourage children to be aware of when they use it. For example, ask in group discussions how many 'pondered' about their problem, or 'recalled' a fairy tale which is similar to *Snow White* in that it involves a wicked witch.
- Display a 'Thought of the Week' which is open for discussion. For example, 'Having money does not make you happy'. Ask children to contribute their thought for others to consider.
- Display and discuss ways of describing thinking.
- Introduce children to mind-maps to help children to categorise and make connections. A key word or image is placed in the centre of a poster (use an object placed on the floor when working with younger children, for example a teddy). Children are encouraged to contribute to the map by adding words/items that link with the original key word or object (next to the teddy, children may add a doll – to fit with the category of toys or a bowl – and spoon – to fit with the story of *The Three Bears*). Use string or card to connect the ideas (older children can do so themselves).
- Leave out the map for children to add and link further ideas.
- Encourage children to give reasons for each idea they contribute.
- Call and Featherstone helpfully elaborate on mind-mapping (32).

Case Study 7.7

Discussing the mind

Children in Year 2 had been thinking about the very difficult subject of 'Our Minds'. They had shared their ideas about what a mind was, what use it was and what it looked like. Some chose to draw a diagram of where the mind was in our body. Their teacher suggested that they think about when they hear people talk about the mind and when they might use the term. She skilfully helped them to come up with the following list and discussed the contexts in which they are used:

> Never mind, do you mind?, did it cross your mind?, mind the puddles, mind the baby, mind out, keep in mind

> *Baba*: '"Never mind" means that you have to throw a worry out of your mind. It mean get rid of it.'

Directly model metacognitive behaviour

Teachers should make their thinking explicit and encourage children to do so (in guided participation). Think aloud – talk about what you are thinking:

> 'The end of term is a really busy time for me; I need to plan carefully what we need to do next week and perhaps make a list.'

Professional checkpoint

Reflect on your own thinking and consider:

- the times at work and at home when you think best
- the conditions which promote your thinking
- the conditions which limit/reduce your thinking.

Share this with children and ask for their reflections.

Links with Parents

How far are your parents aware of the key role that thinking plays in their children's development and learning?
How much do parents understand and value the emphasis placed in school on supporting good thinking?
How do you know?

The impact of metacognition on motivation

The more that children are encouraged to reflect on and use their thought processes at will, the more aware they become of the options they have in approaching a task and setting about solving it. This in turn leads to children feeling in control of their learning, deeply satisfied that, by using their kit of thinking tools, the approach to learning is in their hands. This attitude is the outcome of having a positive mind-set and being a master learner (see Chapter 4). Conversely, those with a limited mind-set may have learned about different thinking processes but will not venture to open their toolkit, preferring to stay with familiar methods (often guessing), even though these methods often prove unsuccessful.

> ## Key points for working with parents
>
> Help parents to recognise the value of sharing their own interests with children.
> Share information with parents about their child's developing thinking competencies and encourage them to listen carefully to their child's comments and questions in order to understand how they convey their thoughts and ideas.
> Suggest that parents:
>
> - encourage their child to write lists of things they need to remember to do and need to think further about
> - ask their child to give reasons for their views, for example, 'So why do you think that going for a walk by the river is really boring?' (this approach will be much more effective if parents in turn justify their views to children).

Useful books

Wilde, Oscar (2006) *Stories for Children*. London: Hodder & Stoughton.
A timeless selection of stories to read to six and seven year olds – all with thought-provoking moral messages.

Rosen, Michael and Blake, Quentin (2007) *Michael Rosen's Sad Book*. London: Walker Books.
A personal reflection on sadness and how the author tries to cope with it. Excellent material for small-group discussions and reflections, particularly with seven year olds.

Browne, Anthony (reprinted 2008) *Piggybook*. London: Walker Books.
A superb story about male chauvinist piggery and how it changes. This provokes discussion about gender roles. Children should scrutinise the pictures carefully to find the many pig images.

References

1. Csikszentmihalyi, M. (1991) 'Thoughts about Education: New Horizons for Learning', quoted in R. House (ed.), *Too Much too Soon*. Gloucester: Hawthorn Press, p. 177.
2. Robinson, K. (2009) *The Element: How Finding Your Passion Changes Everything*. London: Penguin, p. 25.
3. Flynn, J. (2008) 'How to Enhance Your Intelligence', *RSA ejournal*, April, p. 3. Available at: www.thersa.org.uk/journal.
4. Katz, L.G. (1995) *Talks with Teachers of Young Children*. Norwood, NJ: Ablex.

5. Fisher, J. (2010) *Moving on to Key Stage 1*. Maidenhead: Open University Press, pp. 25, 26.

6. Tickell, C. (2010) *The Early Years: Foundations for Life, Health and Learning*. Independent Report to HM Government on the Early Years Foundation Stage. London: Department for Education, pp. 35, 36.

7. NAA (National Assessment Agency) (2008) *Continuing the Learning Journey*. London: Qualification Curriculum Authority, p.19.

8. Sure Start, Department for Education and Skills/Primary National Strategy (2005) *Communicating Matters*. Module 2, Focus 7, pp. 61–2. London: DfES.

9. Fisher (2010) *Moving on to Key Stage 1* (see note 5), p. 96.

10. McGuiness, C. (1999) *From Thinking Skills to Thinking Classrooms*, DfEE Research Brief 115. London: Department for Educaton and Employment (DfEE).

11. Alexander, R. (2004) *Towards Dialogic Thinking: Rethinking Classroom Talk*. Cambridge: Dialogos UK, p. 48.

12. Qualification and Curriculum Authority (QCA)/Department for Education and Skills (2003) *Speaking, Listening and Learning: Working with Children at Key Stage 1 and 2*. London: HMSO, p. 35.

13. Dawes, L. (2006) 'Speaking, Listening and Thinking with Computers', in E. Grugeon, L. Dawes, C. Smith and L. Hubbard (eds), *Teaching Speaking and Listening in the Primary School* (3rd edn). London: David Fulton.

14. Giudici, C., Rinaldi, C. and Krechevsky, M. (2001) *Making Learning Visible: Children as Individual and Group Learners*. Reggio Emilia: Reggio Children.

15. Fisher, R. (1995) *Teaching Children to Think*. Cheltenham: Stanley Thornes, pp. 155–83.

16. Lipman, M. (1982) 'Philosophy for Children', *Thinking: The Journal of Philosophy for Children*, 3: 35–44.

17. Stanley, S. and Bowkett, S. (2008) *But Why? Developing Philosophy in the Classroom*. London: Continuum.

18. Bowles, M. (2008) *Philosophy for Children*. London: A & C Black.

19. Greenfield, G., Gopnik, A. et al. (2011) 'Teach Philosophy in Our Schools', Letter to *The Guardian*, 14 September.

20. McGuiness, C. (2000) *ACTS (Activating Children's Thinking Skills)*, Teaching and Learning Research Programme (TLRP), Economc and Research Council, Queens University, Belfast.

21. Granger, T., Gooch, K. and Lambirth, A. (2002) 'Research in Progress: The Voice of the Child, "We're Writers" Project', *Reading, Literacy and Language*, 36(3), November: 136.

22. Mallett, M. (2003) *Early Years Non-Fiction*. London: Routledge/Falmer, p. 72.

23. Ibid., p. 68.

24. Riley, J. and Reedy, D. (2005) 'Developing Young Children's Thinking through Learning to Write Argument', *Phase One: Classroom Approaches to Developing Young Children's Thinking Skills*. London: NFER, p. 11.

25. Pound, L. and Lee, T. (2011) *Teaching Mathematics Creatively*. Abingdon: Routledge, p. 12.

26. Harlen, W. and Qualter, A. (2009) *The Teaching of Science in the Primary Years* (3rd edn). Abingdon: Routledge, pp. 78–88.

27. Istomina, Z. (1982) 'The Development of Voluntary Memory in Children of Pre-school Age', in U. Nesser (ed.), *Memory Observed: Remembering in Natural Contexts*. San Francisco, CA: Freeman.
28. Swartz, R. and Perkins, D. (1989) 'Teaching Thinking – Issues and Approaches', adapted in R. Fisher (1998) 'Thinking about Thinking: Developing Metacognition in Children', *Early Child Development and Care*, 141: 1–15.
29. Larkin, S. (2010) *Metacognition in Young Children*. Abingdon: Routledge, p. 18.
30. Young Wales (2010) *How To Develop Thinking and Assessment for Learning in the Classroom*. Guidance Document No. 044/2010. Cardiff: Welsh Assembly.
31. Maynard, T., Morgan, A., Waters, J. and Williams, J. (2010) *The Teaching and Learning Research Programme in Wales: The Foundation Stage*. John Furlong (ed.), Teaching and Learning Research Programme (TLRP), Cardiff: Welsh Assembly.
32. Call, N. and Featherstone, S. (2010) *The Thinking Child*. London: Continuum, pp. 109–10.

Index

Added to a page number 'f' denotes a figure and 't' denotes a table.

abandonment 27
abstract thought 5, 32, 33, 37, 138–9
accommodation 16, 18, 74, 139
achievement 15, 92
actions, repetition of 32, 33
Activating Children's Thinking Skills
   (ACTS) 165
active learning 10, 11, 13, 16
adult support
  babies' and infants' thinking 43–68
    climate 55–62
    companionship and communication
      49–55
    during transitions 46–8
    intentional thinking 62–8
    relationships 43–6
  children's thinking 3-5 years 97–124
    climate 112–18
    during transitions 104–7
    intentional thinking 116–24
    relationships 98–103
  children's thinking 5-7 years 152–79
    climate 161–71
    communication and companionship
      160–1
    during transitions 157–9
    intentional thinking 172–9
    relationships 153–7
  young children's thinking
    long-term benefits 9–10
    research evidence 6–7
affording environment 9
Ainsworth, M. 3
Alexander, R. 161
American paediatric study 128
analysing 165, 173
Anning, A. 83, 85, 140
anticipation of events 29–30
anxiety 105
aptitude(s) 130, 131, 153
Arnold, C. 75
assessment 8, 99, 175, 176
assimilation 16, 18, 74, 139
Athey, C. 17, 32, 103, 135
attachment 3, 26–7, 44–5, 71–4
attention deficit 36
attitude(s) 130, 153–4, 178
attunement 40, 43–5
authority 75
authors 140

autonomous learners 15
autonomy 63, 64
awareness
  of other's viewpoints 28–9
  see also metacognitive awareness;
    self-awareness; social awareness;
    spatial awareness

babies' and infants' thinking 25–40
  communication 4, 19, 38–40
  creating imaginary worlds 36–8
  loving relationships 26–7
  receptive brain 25–6
  research evidence 3
  schema 18, 39
  sense making 31–4, 38–9
  social understandings 27–9
  supporting *see* adult support
  world of possibilities 29–31
balance 32
Barnes, D. 144
Bayley, R. 51
behaviour, communication through 38–40
'big C' creativity 81
Birth to Three Matters 3
Bodrova, E. 71, 140
body language 19, 49
books 61
Bowlby, J. 3
boys 80, 139, 148
brain 1–2, 25–6, 29
brain development 52, 97
brief interactions 49
Brierley, J. 97
Broadhead, P. 102
Bromley, H. 114, 140
Bronson, M. 62
Bruce, T. 37, 81, 82, 138
Bruner, J. 19, 31
Building the Curriculum 2 (Scotland) 13

Call, N. 177
cardboard boxes 61
Carey, S. 87
Carr, M. 8, 73
Carrington, V. 79
Carruthers, E. 86, 141
categorisation 40
Characteristics of Effective Teaching and
    Learning 11

checking 115, 148
child-centred approach 117
child-initiated play, observation of 100–1
children
    encouragement of 'in depth' observation
        of 115
    intimate knowledge of individual 98–9
    need to focus on 13–14
Children Thinking Mathematically 86
children's thinking 1–23
    3–5 years 70–93
        communicating, through talk 88–91
        developing dispositions to think 71–4
        sense making 75–88
        social understandings 74–5
        intentional thinking 91–3
    5–7 years 127–49
        intentional thinking 145–9
        maintaining a disposition to think
            129–31
        research 128–9
        sense making 134–43
        sharing and sustaining thinking,
            through talk 144
        social understandings 131–3
    achievement 15
    brain, mind and thought 1–2
    developmental readiness 16
    making connections 16–17
    mental disequilibrium 15–16
    recognising 17–21
    supporting *see* adult support
    upsurge of interest in 2–15
choices 63, 117, 122, 131
classroom environments 176–9
Claxton, G. 2, 7, 8, 73, 81, 129, 144
closed questions 109
co-operation 75, 132
co-operative learning 133
co-operative play 102
Cockburn, A. 140
cognitive development 80, 102, 129,
    132, 146
cognitive self-regulation 71
comments (children's) 19–20
communication 4
    and companionship 49–55, 107–12, 160–1
    and thinking 12
        see also babies' and infant's
            thinking; children's thinking
        see also language; talk
Community of Enquiry 164
companionable apprenticeship 4, 54, 161
companionable attention 4, 46, 49–53,
    153, 160
companionable conversations 4, 49–53,
    154, 160
companionable learning 4
companionable play 4, 46, 53–4, 153, 160
competence, in thinking 14, 128–9
composition 140, 167
computer analogy 2
concentration 146
concepts 18

concrete experiences 5, 139
concrete operations 138
confidence 44, 48, 61, 63, 73, 75, 116, 118
conflict resolution 101–2, 132
connections, making 16–17, 80–2, 130, 140,
    141, 145
connectors (brain) 26
consistency 48
context, and thought 5
contingent care 44
contingent response 50
Continuing the Learning Journey 158
continuous provision 118–19
control 63, 71, 92
conversations *see* companionable
    conversations; musical conversations;
    parentese; peer conversations; rich
    conversations
cortisol 27, 47
counterfactual thinking 30
counting skills 86–7, 114
Craft, A. 81, 110
Crain, W. 65
creating 166
Creating and Thinking Critically 36–7, 81
Creative Development 81
creative ideas 142
creative thinking 11, 36–7, 80–2, 110,
    130, 144
creativity 81, 117
Creativity and Critical Thinking 81
critical thinking 11, 36–7, 130, 164
Csikszentmihalyi, M. 152–3
curiosity 39, 87, 147, 153
Curriculum for Excellence 12

'dance of dialogue' 44
Darwin, C. 40
David, T. 2, 3
Dawes, L. 162
daycare 47–8
decisions 63
deductive thinking 139
defiance 64
dependence 75
*Developing Thinking and Understanding
    in Young Children* 2
development, nurturing 45–6
developmental stages 5, 46
dialogic talk 161–4
dialogue 4, 44, 164
digital technology 80
discovery, through moving and
    sensing 31–3
'discrete' method 6, 7, 161–5
displayed environment 119–20
dispositions to think 7–8
    developing in children 3–5 years 71–4
    maintaining in children 5–7 years 129–31
    strengthening early 8–9
Donaldson, M. 5, 7, 28, 31, 32, 123,
    140, 147
drawing(s) 35, 83, 85, 140, 142
dressing 64

Duckworth, A. 72
Dundee research group 50, 52
Dunn, J. 28, 74, 131, 132
Dweck, C. 8, 72, 73

Early Education Projects on Young Children
    Thinking 13
Early Excellence 118–19
Early Years Foundation Stage (EYFS) 11,
    75t, 81
Early Years National Frameworks
    10–11
Effective Provision of Pre-School Education
    (EPPE) project 9–10, 45
Element (being in the) 15, 129–31
    adult support 153–6
Elkind, D. 36
emotional self-regulation 71
empathy 28, 132, 166
enactive representation(s) 19, 31
'enclosing' schema 33, 34, 75t, 76
encouragement 123
England 10, 11–12, 147
enquiry/enquiring 40, 115, 166
'enveloping' schema 33, 75t, 76
environment
    dispositions to think 8–9
    infant awareness 32
    infant exploration 27
    thinking-friendly 118–19
    using displayed 119–20
    see also classroom environments; literacy
        focused environments; natural
        environment; rich environments
Epstein, A. 92
equilibrium 16, 18
equivalence 141
evaluation/evaluating 92, 166, 173t
evaluative memory 122
Every Child a Talker 112
everyday creativity 81
*Excellence and Enjoyment: Learning and
    Teaching in the Primary Years* 147
expectations, development of 145–6
experience(s)
    development and enriched 140
    infant's receptive brain 26
    making sense of second-hand 35–6
    re-presentations of 19
    self-regulation and 92
    shared 102
    see also concrete experiences; home
        experiences; physical experiences; rich
        experiences
experiential thinking 161
exploration 11, 27, 56, 72, 87, 97
exploratory play 56, 136
exploratory talk 144, 164
expression (of thought) 166
Expressive Arts and Design 12, 81
eye contact 19

facial expressions 28
fairness 132

fantasy play *see* pretend and fantasy play
Featherstone, S. 177
feelings 27, 28–9, 72
Fernyhough, C. 77
Fisher, J. 128, 136, 142, 145, 147
fixed mind-sets 72, 105, 130
flashcards 64–5
flexible thinking 30
Flynn, J. 155
formal thinking 5
Foundation Phase Framework for Children's
    Learning (Wales) 12
friendships 74, 75, 101, 102, 131–2, 157
Froebel Early Education Project 17, 32, 103
frustration(s) 39, 73, 130, 153
functional dependency level, schema
    operations 33

games 51, 53, 61, 123
gender 80, 139, 148
'generalised event representations' 76
Gerba, M. 65
Gerhardt, S. 3, 26, 65
gestures 19, 49
giftedness 173
'give and take' games 53
Goddard Blythe, S. 40
'going concerns' 62, 63
Goldschmeid, E. 52, 56
Gopnik, A. 1, 29, 30, 37, 65, 82
graphic representations 83–5
graphics, mathematical 86, 114
Greenfield, S. 1
greetings 98
Grenier, J. 98, 101, 138
group work 162
grouping 40
groups, thinking in 157
growth mind-set 72, 73, 129, 153
The Guardian 165
guided participation 4, 161, 178

'habits of mind' 7, 8
Hall, N. 89, 140
Hare Brain, Tortoise Mind 81
Hargreaves, D. 9
Harlen, W. 142, 169
Haylock, D. 140
helpless behaviour 72, 73
Helwig, C. 131
heuristic play 56–7
High Scope 123
higher level thinking 5
home, influence of 10
home experiences 79–80
home literacy environment 51
home visits 98
Hope, G. 38
Hughes, M. 89
The Hundred Languages of Children 88
hypothesising 56, 144

iconic representation 19
ideas 38, 82, 142, 169, 170

ideas books 168
identity 27
illumination 82
imaginary worlds 36–8
imagination 65, 78, 80, 141
imaginative play 37, 136
imitation 28, 36, 37, 54, 97
inborn growth schedule 65–6
inclusion 11
incubation, creative thinking 81
independence, supporting
    63–4, 117
inductive thinking 139
infants *see* babies and infants
information processing 142, 144, 165
informational approach, supporting
    intentional thinking 117
'infusion' method 6, 7, 165–6, 167
integrated age groups 54
intellectual capacity 65
intellectual search 89, 97
intentional behaviour 39
intentional thinking
    children 3–5 years 91–3
        adult support 116–24
    children 5–7 years 145–9
        adult support 172–9
    encouraging early 62–8
intentions, awareness of others' 28–9
interactive displays 120
interests (children's) 11, 14, 15, 17, 59–60,
    66, 130
internal dialogue 4
investigation 29, 57, 72, 83, 169
inviting environment 9
involvement 73, 130
Isaacs, S. 87
'island of intimacy' 53

Journal of the Royal Society of Arts 155
justice 132

Karmiloff-Smith, A. 91
Katz, L. 7, 155
key persons 3, 18, 27, 28, 44, 46, 48,
    52, 53, 65, 71, 103, 122
Key Stage 1, supporting transition
    to 157–9
know how 147
knowledge
    of each child 98–9
    reflection and 92
'known items', treasure baskets 57
Kress, G. 83

Laevers, F. 73
Lafferty, P. 123
language
    communication through 4, 38–40
    development 88
    in mathematics 141
    and thought 12
Larkin, S. 173
Leach, P. 47

learning
    companionable 4
    effective 11
    opportunities for 11
    screen-based 36
    slower ways of 81
    and thinking 2
learning journeys 105
Learning, Playing and Interacting 80
Learning Stories 8
Lee, T. 141, 168
Leong, D.J. 71, 140
Let's Think 7
letters 85
lifelong learning 11
Linn, S. 81
listening to children 20, 65, 66, 98–100
lists 168
literacy 10
literacy focused environments 51
'little c' creativity 81
locations, adult support in thinking
    about 115
looking time 28–9
Louis, S. 34
loving relationships 26–7

McGuiness, C. 6, 7, 161, 165
McTavish, A. 101
Mallett, M. 167, 168
management style, supporting intentional
    thinking 117–18
Manning Morton, J. 26
maps 84–5
mark making 19, 35, 83–5, 114
Mark Making Matters 86
markers 89
Marsh, J. 79
mastery 64, 72, 73
mathematical graphics 86, 114
mathematical thinking 12
    children 3–5 years 86–7
        adult support 114–15
    children 5–7 years 140–1
        adult support 168–9
Matthews, J. 35, 83
maturation 71
meaning making *see* sense making
measures, understanding of 87, 114
Meggitt, C. 138
memory 105, 122, 146
mental disequilibrium 15–16, 74
mental environments (rich) 155
metacognition
    children 3–5 years 92
        adult support 123–4
    children 5–7 years 147–9
        adult support 176–9
metacognitive awareness 172–4
mime 40
mind(s) 1–2, 6, 132
mind maps 177
mind-sets 71–4, 105, 130, 178
Mindsets 8

mistakes 91, 116, 122, 154
modelling, metacognitive behaviour 178
moral understandings 131–2
motivation, metacognition and 178
movement 31–3, 55–6, 83
Moylett, H. 4
music 40, 44, 83
musical conversations 40, 44

National Curriculum 2, 10, 19, 135
National Foundation of Educational
    Research (NFER) 6, 128–9, 168
National Frameworks, children's
    thinking in 10–13
National Strategies 80, 83, 112
natural environment 56
natural materials, contact with 115
nature/nurture question 25–6
negative self-esteem 72–3
neuroscience 3, 64
New Zealand Council for Educational
    Research 49
non-fiction writing 168
non-verbal communication 39, 65
Northern Ireland 10, 13, 128
Nutbrown, C. 64
Nuttall, G. 135

object permanence 30–1, 37, 46, 51
observation (adult) 57, 62, 63, 65, 98–101
observation (child) 87, 115
open questions 109
open-framework approach, supporting
    intentional thinking 117
opportunities
    for peer assessment 176
    for thinking and learning 11, 130,
        131, 154–7
others' minds, thinking about 132
other's viewpoints, awareness of 28–9
Owen, S. 65

Page, J. 64
Pahl, K. 34
painting 35
paints 61
pair work 132
Paley, V. 78, 80
Palmer, S. 51
parentese 44–5
parenting, and communication 50–1
parents, relationships with 103
passion 130, 153
passivity 27
pedagogy 167
peek-a-boo games 51, 61
Peel, E.A. 2
peer assessment 176
peer collaboration 133
peer conversations 20–1
peer modelling 133
peer support 80, 133
peer tutoring 133
Penn Green Centre 75

pens 61
person permanence 31, 46, 51
personal, social and emotional development
    12, 92
personalised contacts 51
Petrie, S. 65
Philosophy for Children 7, 164–6
physical development 12
physical experiences 31
Piaget, J. 5, 16, 32, 131, 138
planning play 122
play
    and creative thinking 81
    effective teaching and learning 11
    media and popular culture 79–80
    observation of child-initiated 100–1
    planning 122
    practitioner participation 99
    and schemes of thinking 17
    and social understanding 74
    see also companionable play; heuristic
        play; imaginative play; pretend and
        fantasy play; role play; social play
playfulness 73
pointing 27, 40
pole-bridge talk 51–2
popular culture 79–80, 113–14, 137–8
'positioning' schema 33, 75t
positive mind-set 178
positive self-esteem 71
possibilities, the world of 29–31
possibility questions 110
potentiating environment 9
Pound, L. 141, 168
practitioners
    and children's thinking
        beliefs and practices 9
        increased insights in day-to-day
            work 13–15
    see also adult support
praise 123
pre-frontal cortex 29
prediction 30, 92, 115, 123, 148, 169
preparation, creative thinking 81
presentational talk 144
pretend and fantasy play
    babies and infants 37–8
        adult support 53, 61
    children 3–5 years 77–9
        adult support 112–13
    children 5–7 years 136–8
        adult support 167
Primary Framework for Literacy 10
private spaces 61
private speech 92, 121
problem finding 110
problem solving 5, 10–11, 64, 101, 110, 147–8
programmed approach 65, 117
prohibiting environment 9

Qualter, A. 169
questions/questioning
    adult 109–10, 160, 175–6
    children's 19–20, 89, 110–11

re-enacting 80–1
Read, V. 105
reading, in play 136
reasoning 132, 139, 140, 165, 173
recall 122
receptive brain 25–6
receptive language 89
reciprocity 37, 73
reconstruction 37
recording mathematics 86
reflection 92, 147, 175–6
Reggio Emilia schools 88, 107, 162
relationships
    adult support
        babies and infants 43–6
        children 3–5 years 98–103
        children 5–7 years 153–7
    as key to smooth transitions 104–7
    see also attachment; social relationships;
        special person relationship
repetition, of actions 32, 33
representations 19, 31, 80–1
    adult support 61, 62f
    'generalised event' 76
    see also mark-making; writing
repression of feelings 27
research, children's thinking 3–10
Researching Effective Pedagogy in the Early
    Years (REPEY) 9–10
resilience 73
resources 34–5, 118–19
responsibility 9, 115, 117, 145
rich child 107
rich conversations 89
rich environments 16, 51, 107, 155
rich experiences 29, 32, 56, 81
Ring, K. 83, 85, 140
rituals (questioning) 160
Roberts, R. 4
Robinson, K. 129, 131, 153
Robinson, M. 1, 25, 44, 45
Robson, S. 2, 9, 19, 81, 87, 92, 102
Rogoff, B. 4
role play 14, 16, 32, 119, 167
role rehearsal 37
'rotating' schema 33, 75t
rough and tumble play 80
routines 48, 53, 76

schema 17–18
    consolidating and extending 75–6
    development, leading to later concepts 134–6
    disputes, and conflicting 75
    early 32–4, 39
    provision for 57–8
    shared understandings about children's 103
schema cluster 76
schematic interests 56, 66
scientific thinking
    babies and infants 32
    children 3–5 years 87, 88
        adult support 115–16
    children 5–7 years 142–3
        adult support 168–70

Scotland 10, 12–13, 127
screen-based media
    development of fantasy play
        137–8
    harnessing thinking derived from
        113–14
    merits and dangers for babies and
        infants 36
    provision for interests 59–60
    sense making 35–6, 79–80
scribbles 83
scripts (social) 76–7
second-hand experiences, making sense
    of 35–6
secure attachments 27, 46, 47
secure base 3, 27, 46
self-awareness 147
self-belief 71, 72
self-esteem 71, 72–3
self-evaluation 147
self-knowledge 71, 147
self-regulation
    babies and infants 39
        adult support 62
    children 3–5 years 70–1, 92
        adult support 116–17, 121–2
    children 5–7 years 145
        adult support 172
self-talk 39
sense making 5
    babies and infants 26, 31–6, 38–9
        adult support 55–60
    children 3–5 years 75–88
        adult support 112
    children 5–7 years 134–43
        adult support 161–71
sensing
    discovery through 31–3
    provision for 55–6
sensorimotor level, schema
    operations 32
separateness 27–8
shape, understanding of 87, 114
shared experiences 102
shared reading 51, 168
shared thinking 74, 75
Siegler, R. 72
Sigman, A. 36
signing 49
social awareness 144
social constructivists 62
social contacts 3–4, 65, 74
Social and Emotions Aspects of Development
    (SEAD) 98
social engagement 40
social intelligence 131
social interactions 88
social learning 74
social play 120
social reference 27
social relationships 3–4, 74
social scripts 76–7
social sensitivity 145–6
social skills 89, 149, 165

social understandings
  babies and infants 27–9
  children 3–5 years 74–5
  children 5–7 years 131–3
sounds 49
space
  adult support in thinking about 114, 115
  for incubating ideas 81
  private 61
  understanding of 87
spatial awareness 32
special person relationship 47, 48
special persons 27, 53, 54, 58, 63, 64, 98, 153, 155
speculation, fostering 115
stage theories 5
standards, development of 145–6
stories 61, 77, 78, 85
stress 27, 65, 92, 105
super-hero play 80, 113–14, 136
support see adult support
surprise 56
surroundings 83–4
sustained endeavours, supporting 122–4
sustained interactions 49–50
sustained shared thinking 4, 10, 13
sustained thinking, supporting 122–4
symbol systems 83, 85, 139
symbolic level, schema operations 32
symbolic representation 19
symbolic thinking 161
symbols, use of 19, 37

talk
  about thinking, suggested vocabulary 174–5
  communicating thoughts through 88–91
  sharing and sustaining thinking through 144, 162
  supporting 108–9
  see also conversations; dialogic talk; dialogue; pole-bridge talk; private speech; self-talk
Talking partners 157
tallies 114
Teletubbies 36
television, and attention deficit 36
temper tantrums 40
testing 32, 56, 57, 80, 142
theory of mind 27, 37
thinking see babies' and infant's thinking; children's thinking
thinking aloud 178
thinking friends 157
thinking processes 166, 174–5, 177
thinking skills 2, 7–8, 10, 165–6
thinking words 177
thinking-friendly environment 118–19
thought in action 31

Thought of the Week 177
Tickell Review 11–12, 36–7, 70–1, 92, 158
time, allowing 64–7, 112, 164
Tizard, B. 89
tongues, infant use of 55
Tools of the Mind 122
'trajectory' schema 33, 75t
transaction, writing development 140
transcribing 83, 140
transformation 141, 142
transitional objects 47
transitions
  adult support during
    babies and infants 46–8
    children 5–7 years 157–9
    young children 3–5 years 104–7
  ages of 127–8
  friendships and 131
'transporting' schema 33
treasure bags 56
treasure baskets 56
Trevarthen, C. 40, 49
trial-and-error approach, to problem solving 148
Turiel, E. 131
turn-taking 51

Understanding the World 87–8, 115–16

verbal thinking 39
verification 82
video cameras 103
viewpoints, awareness of others' 28–9
visual displays 177
vocabulary 39
Vygotsky, L. 3, 74–5, 83, 88, 122, 132, 136, 147

Wales 10, 12, 127, 147, 157, 174
Wallas, G. 81
Weinstein, N. 80
well-being (children's) 4, 15, 73, 102, 130
Wellbeing from Birth 4
White, J. 56
Whitehead, M. 34, 39
Why Love Matters 26
Winnicott, D. 47
Wood, D. 5, 146
working memory 105
worry 105
Worthington, M. 86, 141
writing
  children 3–5 years 85
  children 5–7 years 136, 140
    adult support 167–8
  as a secondary symbol system 83

young children's thinking see children's thinking